The Plutarch Project

Volume Five

Alexander and Timoleon

by

Anne E. White

The Plutarch Project Volume Five: Alexander and Timoleon
Copyright © 2019 by Anne E. White www.annewrites.ca

Cover photograph and cover design: Bryan White

All rights reserved. No part of this publication may be reproduced, stored in a retrieval system or transmitted in any form by any means, electronic, mechanical, photocopy, recording or otherwise, without the prior permission of the publisher, except as provided by Canadian copyright law.

ISBN 978-0-9958889-2-0

CONTENTS

Introduction 1

Alexander III of Macedon 3

    Lesson One 9

    Lesson Two 14

    Lesson Three 19

    Lesson Four 24

    Lesson Five 29

    Lesson Six 35

    Lesson Seven 38

    Lesson Eight 41

    Lesson Nine 45

    Lesson Ten 50

    Lesson Eleven 54

    Lesson Twelve 59

    Examination Questions for Term One 63

    Lesson Thirteen 65

    Lesson Fourteen 69

    Lesson Fifteen 73

    Lesson Sixteen 77

    Lesson Seventeen 81

    Lesson Eighteen 87

Lesson Nineteen 90

Lesson Twenty 97

Lesson Twenty-One 100

Lesson Twenty-Two 104

Lesson Twenty-Three 107

Lesson Twenty-Four... 112

Examination Questions for Term Two 116

Timoleon 117

Lesson One... 121

Lesson Two 124

Lesson Three.. 129

Lesson Four 133

Lesson Five 138

Lesson Six 143

Lesson Seven.. 148

Lesson Eight 153

Lesson Nine 157

Lesson Ten 161

Lesson Eleven 166

Lesson Twelve.. 170

Examination Questions.. 175

Bibliography 176

Introduction

These notes, and the accompanying text, are prepared for the use of individual students and small groups following a twelve-week term. The text is that of Thomas North's 1579 translation of Plutarch's *Lives of the Noble Greeks and Romans*, with substitutions from John Dryden's 1683 translation [in brackets]. I have updated spelling and punctuation. Omissions for length and/or suitability are noted.

Using the Lesson Material

Each study contains explanatory material before the first lesson. A little at the beginning may be useful to stir interest in the study, but it is not meant to be given all in one dose!

Some lessons are divided into two or three sections. These can be read all at once or used throughout the week.

I encourage you to make the lessons your own. Use the questions that are the most meaningful to you. Remember that Charlotte Mason was satisfied with "Proper names are written on the blackboard, and then the children narrate what they have listened to."

Examination Questions

The two studies in this volume include suggestions for end-of-term examinations, with separate questions for each term of the *Life of Alexander*. The questions were drawn from original P.N.E.U. programmes.

A note of thanks

I am very grateful to the homeschooling families who field-tested these lessons.

Alexander III of Macedon (356-323 B.C.)

"Another time also when he was in Spain, reading the history of Alexander's acts, when he had read it, he was sorrowful a good while after, and then burst out in weeping. His friends, seeing that, marvelled what should be the cause of his sorrow. 'Do ye not think,' said he, 'that I have good cause to be heavy, when King Alexander being no older than myself is now, had in old time won so many nations and countries: and that I hitherunto have done nothing worthy of myself?'" (Plutarch's *Life of Julius Caesar*)

Alexander the Great may be the best known and the most romanticized of Plutarch's biographical subjects. His story has been examined and debated for over two thousand years, by everyone from Oxford scholars to schoolchildren making stop-motion videos. Although Alexander lived only a few hundred years before this account was written, and historians had described his life in detail, Plutarch still had to deal with unconfirmed stories and questionable "facts," from the legends around Alexander's birth to his mysterious death. However, Plutarch was concerned largely with character, moral choices, and the problems of leadership and government. Does power always corrupt? Should kings live in safety and luxury, or should they fight on the front lines? What motivates greatness? (What *is* greatness?)

Who was Alexander?

Alexander was born into the Macedonian royal family in 356 B.C. For many years, the dominant political power in Europe and the Middle East had been the Persian empire; but Persia's strength had weakened, and its subjects were becoming rebellious. Alexander's father, Philip II of Macedon, became king soon after his son was born, and he was credited with reforming and strengthening the army (using the famous phalanx formation). He planned to combine Macedon's military power with that of the Greek states, and to attack Persia (**Lesson Two**).

Philip's assassination in 336 left that ambition unfulfilled. However, his son Alexander spent the next thirteen years conquering a previously undreamed-of share of the world.

Is it Macedon or Macedonia? Were the Macedonians Greeks?

The names are used interchangeably. Macedonia, or Macedon, was a kingdom in the northeastern part of mainland Greece. The Macedonians were Greek in many respects, such as religious beliefs; but they valued their distinct heritage and identity.

What is meant by "barbarous?"

The word "barbarous" meant "foreign" or "not Greek." It carried overtones of "strange," but it did not imply "savage or cruel."

People in this Story

Alexander's Teachers

Aristotle: "The Father of Western Philosophy" was hired by King Philip to teach Alexander (and other young men) subjects such as natural philosophy (science) and rhetoric.

Leonidas of Epirus: Alexander's schoolmaster and a relative of his mother Olympias.

Lysimachus of Acarnania: Alexander's second-place tutor, who suggested the nicknames "Phoenix" for himself, "Achilles" for Alexander, and "Peleus" for Philip.

Anaxarchus: one of the philosophers called to counsel Alexander during his grief after killing Clitus (**Lesson Seventeen**).

Alexander's Military Colleagues

Nearchus/Nearchos: Alexander's chief admiral and official explorer.

Parmenio/Parmenion: Philip's chief lieutenant, and later a general to Alexander. His eldest son was **Philotas**, a cavalry commander.

Perdiccas: one of Alexander's generals, later the head of the Imperial Army, and regent during the reign of Alexander's half-brother **Arrhidaeus** (see note below).

Antipater was born in 397 B.C. He appears in **Lesson Three** as "one of Alexander's chiefest servants." Antipater was an advisor and friend to Alexander, and to Alexander's mother **Olympias**, during the early years of his reign, and he acted as regent (substitute ruler) when Alexander was in Persia and India. His friendship with Alexander gradually deteriorated, due to mistrust and jealousy.

Antipater's son **Cassander** is not mentioned until **Lesson Twenty-Three**. He lived from about 350-297 B.C., and later became king of Macedon. As a boy, he had been a student of Aristotle along with Alexander. A conflict between Cassander's own son (also named Alexander) and Demetrius is described in Plutarch's *Life of Demetrius*.

Plutarch also mentions another of Antipater's sons, **Iolaus**, who was suspected of poisoning Alexander.

Antigonus Monopthalmus (or "Antigonus with One Eye"): Those who have read the *Life of Demetrius* will remember Antigonus, the father of Demetrius and one of Alexander's generals.

Seleucus I Nicator was a general in Alexander's army who eventually ruled much of the Middle East. He is, however, barely mentioned in this story. **Ptolemy I Soter**, another general, became ruler of Egypt after Alexander's death. He is also not mentioned much here.

The Wives and Children of Alexander

Alexander had a complicated list of marriages and other relationships. The most important to know are his wives **Statira** (also spelled **Stateira**) and **Roxane** (also **Roxana** or **Rhoxane**). A third wife was named **Parysatis**. Alexander is believed to have been the father of at least two sons, including Alexander IV of Macedon, who was born to **Roxane** after his death.

Other People

Cleopatra Eurydice was a stepmother to Alexander.

Arrhidaeus: Alexander's half-brother became King Philip Arrhidaeus III of Macedon in 323 B.C. According to historians, he was not considered fully capable of ruling, possibly due to a childhood injury. He was put to death by Alexander's mother **Olympias**.

Hephaestion: one of Alexander's closest friends. Some thought that Alexander's grief over Hephaestion's death hastened his own end.

Craterus: another of Alexander's generals

Darius III: king of Persia at the time

Harpalus: Those who have read the *Life of Demosthenes* will remember Alexander's friend Harpalus, whose visit to Athens (while escaping Alexander's anger) caused trouble for Demosthenes. (Those events are mentioned briefly here in **Lesson Fifteen**.)

How P.N.E.U. teachers taught *Alexander*

There are a few mentions of the *Life of Alexander* in Charlotte Mason's writings and in early *Parents' Review* articles. Interestingly, it appears under the subjects of both Narration/Language and History, but not Citizenship (its place in later P.N.E.U. programmes).

Two lesson plans for passages in *Alexander* appear in Appendix V of *School Education*, "How Oral Lessons are Used." The first lesson is designed to take twenty minutes, and the second, thirty; the first says that it is intended for students with an average age of ten, and the other is for students aged eight or nine (below the usual age for Plutarch in the later programmes).

The first lesson plan (included below) is the simplest. Note **Step 2**, which sounds like Charlotte Mason's Bible lessons as described in *Home Education*, giving students an overview of the story before reading the whole thing. Elsewhere, we are directed to read a passage without much preamble and let the students take from it what they can, rather than kill the story with too much talk. However, telling the story-before-the-story is a way to unlock difficult passages, or those that include significant events such as famous battles.

> **Step 1.** Connect with the last lesson by questioning the children. They read last time stories illustrating Alexander's graciousness and tact.
> **Step 2.** Tell the children shortly the substance of what I am going to read to them, letting them find any places mentioned, in their maps.
> **Step 3.** Read to the children about three pages, dealing with the luxury of the Macedonians, Alexander's march to Bactria, and the death of Darius. Read this slowly and distinctly, and "into" the children as much as possible.
> **Step 4.** Ask the children in turn to narrate, each narrating a part of what was read.

The second lesson is longer, but as it is also included in *School Education*, I will not repeat it here. This was intended as a first lesson on Alexander, "a fresh hero." After discussing a few details about place and time, the class read and narrated the story of Alexander's taming of Bucephalus. They were asked to list "the qualities which go to make a hero," and looked for examples of those qualities in the story. The teacher pointed out that Alexander himself admired heroic qualities (seen in his admiration for *The Iliad*), and she stressed the impact of Alexander's life on the world.

Charlotte Mason notes, "These [oral] lessons are always expansions or illustrations or summaries of some part of the scholars' current bookwork." In other words, they were not written to show how every lesson should be studied, including Plutarch; but as reminders of the aim to teach with "things and ideas," and as suggestions of ways that books written for adults may be used with young students, without either patronizing them or confusing them with irrelevancies.

Maps and Alexander's World

Because Alexander's story covers such a broad range of places, it is helpful to refer to maps in a historical atlas or the online equivalent. This study contains extra notes under the heading "On the Map."

Top Ten Terms in *Alexander*

If you recognize these words, you're well on your way to mastering North's vocabulary. (They will not be noted in the lessons.)

1. **Acquaint: To acquaint** is used several times in the story, meaning either "to become used to, familiar with" or "to share information."

2. **Choler:** anger, temper

3. **Divers:** several

4. **Footmen:** foot soldiers

5. **Physic:** medicine, both the science and the potion. An expert in medicine is a **physician**.

6. **Repair unto:** go to, turn to

7. **Spoil** or **spoils:** items seized from an enemy; loot

8. **Stay:** delay, detain, stop

9. **Strange:** usually means "foreign," but sometimes it just means "strange." Soldiers that are **strangers** are often foreign mercenaries (soldiers employed by any army that will pay them).

10. **Target:** shield

   (Bonus word: victuals (pronounced vittles): food.)

Lesson One

Introduction

What do your students know already about Alexander the Great? Do they have any ideas about how he earned that title?

In two sample lessons included in Charlotte Mason's book *School Education* (see the introductory notes for this study), an unnamed teacher describes Alexander's "wisdom, valour, and self-reliance," and his "love of simplicity, generosity, and kindness to his men." She suggests that Alexander had a gift of prudence, and that he knew how to put important things first. As you read this *Life* for yourself, you may agree that those traits accurately describe Alexander throughout his life; or you may argue that his values were changed by events and circumstances. (Did Alexander retain his love of simplicity, or was it destroyed when he began to dress like a Persian?) Or you may disagree with them completely. (Was Alexander truly wise and great?)

Vocabulary

counterfeit: in this context, it means to reproduce

chaste: this usually refers to sexual purity, but it refers here to moderation in other matters such as eating

playing at the staff: fighting with staffs or sticks (like Robin Hood)

ought worth: worth anything

occasion: opportunity

churlish: unpleasant, rude

yerk: jerk, kick

jeopard[ize]: bet, wager

voice a-good: Dryden, "in a commanding voice"

was lighted from: alighted from, got down from

People

Philip, Parmenio, etc.: see introductory notes for this study

Lysippus, Appeles: artists who sculpted and painted Alexander

Historic Occasions

357 B.C.: marriage of Olympias and Philip (Alexander's parents)

356 B.C.: birth of Alexander

346 B.C.: Alexander tamed Bucephalus

On the Map

On a map of Europe and Asia, preferably one representing the fourth century B.C., locate Macedon and the Persian Empire.

Reading

Part One

[*omission: omens pertaining to Alexander's birth*]

Shortly after **King Philip** had won the city of Potidaea, three

Alexander

messengers came to him the same day that brought him great news. The first [was] that **Parmenio** had won a notable battle of the Illyrians: the second, that his horse [had won the course] at the Olympian games: and the third, that his wife had brought him a son called Alexander. Philip being marvellous glad to hear these news, the soothsayers did make his joy yet greater: assuring him that his son which was born with three victories all together should be invincible.

Now for [Alexander's] stature and personage, the statues and images made of him by **Lysippus** do best declare it, for that he would be drawn of no man but him only. Divers of his successors and friends did afterwards **counterfeit** his image, but that excellent workman Lysippus only, of all other[s] the chiefest, hath perfectly drawn and resembled Alexander's manner of holding his neck somewhat hanging down towards the left side, and also the sweet look and cast of his eyes [*Dryden: his melting eye*]. But when **Apelles** painted Alexander holding lightning in his hand, he did not shew his fresh colour, but made him somewhat [browner and darker] than his face indeed was: for naturally he had a very fair white colour, mingled also with red, which chiefly appeared in his face and in his breast.

[*omission*]

This natural heat that Alexander had, made him (as it appeareth) to be given to drink, and to be hasty. [But] even from his childhood they saw that he was given to be **chaste**. For though otherwise he was very hot and hasty, yet was he hardly moved with lust or pleasure of the body and would moderately use it.

But on the other side, the ambition and desire he had of honour, shewed a certain coveted greatness of mind and noble courage, passing his years. For he was not (as his father Philip) desirous of all kind[s] of glory: who, like a rhetorician, had a delight to utter his eloquence, and stamped in his coins the victories he had won at the Olympian games by the swift running of his horse and coaches. For when he was asked one day (because he was swift of foot) whether he would essay to run for victory at the Olympian games: "I could be content," said he, "[if] I might run with kings." And yet to speak generally, he misliked all such contention for games. For it seemeth that he utterly misliked all wrestling and other exercise for prize[s], where men did use all their strength: but otherwise he himself made certain festival days and games of prize, for common stage players, musicians, and singers, and for the very poets also. He delighted also in hunting of divers kinds of beasts, and **playing at the staff**.

Part Two

Ambassadors being sent on a time from the king of Persia, whilst his father was in some journey out of his realm: Alexander, familiarly entertaining of them, so won them with his courteous entertainment (for he used no childish questions unto them, nor asked them trifling matters, but what distance it was from one place to another, and which way they went into the high countries of Asia, and of the king of Persia himself, how he was towards his enemies, and what power he had), that he did ravish them with delight to hear him; insomuch that they made no more account of Philip's eloquence and sharp wit, in respect of his son's courage and noble mind to attempt great enterprises.

For when they brought him news that his father had taken some famous city, or had won some great battle, he was nothing glad to hear it, but would say to his playfellows: "Sirs, my father will have all, I shall have nothing left me to conquer with you, that shall be **ought worth**." For he, delighting neither in pleasure nor riches, but only in valiantness and honour, thought that the greater conquests and realms his father should leave him, the less he should have to do for himself. And therefore, seeing that his father's dominions and empire increased daily more and more, perceiving all **occasion** taken from him to do any great attempt: he desired no riches nor pleasure, but wars and battles, and aspired to a [realm] where he might win honour.

He had divers men appointed him (as it is to be supposed) to bring him up: as schoolmasters, governors, and grooms of his chamber to attend upon him: and among those, **Leonidas** was the chiefest man that had the government and charge of him, a man of a severe disposition, and a kinsman also unto **Queen Olympias**. He misliked to be called a master or tutor, though it be an office of good charge; whereupon the others called him Alexander's governor, because he was a noble man, and allied to the prince. But he that bare the name of his schoolmaster was **Lysimachus**, an Acarnanian born, who had no other manner of civility in him saving that he called himself

"Phoenix," Alexander "Achilles," and Philip "Peleus": and therefore, he was well thought of, and was the second person next unto Leonidas.

Part Three

At what time Philonicus [the] Thessalian had brought Bucephalus the horse to sell unto King Philip, asking thirteen talents, they went into the field to ride him. The horse was found so rough and **churlish** that the riders said he would never do service, for he would let no man get up on his back, nor abide any of the gentlemen's voices about King Philip; but would **yerk** out at them. Thereupon, Philip being afraid, commanded them to carry him away as a wild beast, and altogether unprofitable: the which they [would have] done, had not Alexander that stood by said, "Gods, what a horse do they turn away, for lack of skill and heart to handle him." Philip heard what he said but held his peace. Alexander, oft repeating his words, seem[ed] to be sorry that they should send back the horse again. "Why," said Philip, "dost thou control them that have more experience than thou, and that know better than thou how to handle a horse?" Alexander answered, "And yet methinks I should handle him better than all they have done." "But if thou canst not, no more than they," replied Philip: "what wilt thou forfeit for thy folly?" "I am content," (quoth Alexander) "to **jeopard[ize]** the price of the horse." Every man laughed to hear his answer, and the wager was laid between them. Then ran Alexander to the horse and took him by the bridle and turned him towards the sun. It seemed that he had marked (as I suppose) how mad the horse was to see his own shadow, which was ever before him in his eye, as he stirred to and fro. Then Alexander speaking gently to the horse, and clapping him on the back with his hand, till he had left his fury and snorting: softly let fall his cloak from him, and lightly leaping on his back, got up without any danger, and holding the reins of the bridle hard, without striking or stirring the horse, made him to be gentle enough. Then when he saw that the fury of the horse was past, and that he began to gallop, he put him to his full career, and laid on spurs and voice a-good. Philip at the first with fear beholding his son's agility, lest he should take some hurt, said never a word: but when he saw him readily turn the horse at the end of his career, in a bravery for that he had done, all the lookers on gave a shout for joy. The father, on the other side (as they say), fell a-weeping for joy. And when Alexander **was lighted from** the horse, he said unto him, kissing his head: "O son, thou must needs have a realm that is meet for thee, for Macedon will not hold thee."

[After this, considering Alexander to be of a temper easy to be led to his duty by reason, but by no means to be compelled, Philip always endeavoured to persuade rather than to command or to force him to anything.]

Narration and Discussion

Retell the story of Alexander and Bucephalus. (**Creative alternative:** choose another point of view from which to tell the story.) Why do you think this story has been retold so often? What does it say about Alexander's character, even as a boy?

"He desired no riches nor pleasure, but wars and battles." Should we admire Alexander's determination to make his country great?

For older students: How does the last sentence compare Philip's education of Alexander to Alexander's management of the horse? Is this a useful philosophy for those who lead or train others?

Lesson Two

Introduction

As Alexander grew up, he received his schooling, put down a rebellion, and suddenly became king of Macedon. He seemed to have had the perfect education and training, but he was still very young. Was he prepared to handle this new role?

Vocabulary

    affiance: trust

    honourable stipend: generous pay

Alexander

ambitious humour: desire to be greater than all others

published and not published: Aristotle explained that yes, he had published the metaphysical teaching which had been only for the privileged; but there was no danger in making that knowledge public, because most people wouldn't understand it anyway.

memoranda: reminders; something to refresh one's knowledge

knowledge of speculation: abstract, theoretical knowledge

given to his book: a lover of reading

casket copy: see **Lesson Nine** for an explanation of the "casket"

allured: tempted, persuaded

People

Aristotle, Harpalus: see introductory notes

Pausanius of Orestis: one of Philip's bodyguards. The story of his personal grudge has been told by other historians, but it cannot be repeated here. Briefly, he blamed Philip for not avenging an insult that he had received. The mystery around the murder seems to be who it was that persuaded Pausanias to carry it out; even Alexander was not above suspicion.

Historic Occasions

343 B.C.: Aristotle became Alexander's teacher

338 B.C.: Battle of Chaeronea

Summer, 336 B.C.: Darius III became king of Persia

October, 336 B.C.: Alexander became king of Macedon

On the Map

Locate Chaeronea and Thebes.

Reading

Part One

Now Philip put no great **affiance** in [the] schoolmasters of music and humanity for the instruction and education of his son whom he had appointed to teach him; but [he thought] rather that he needed men of greater learning than their capacities would reach unto: and that as Sophocles sayeth,

> He needed many reins, and many bits at once [Dryden: *"the bridle and the rudder too"*].

He sent for **Aristotle** (the greatest philosopher in his time, and best learned) to teach his son, unto whom he gave **honourable stipend**.

[short omission]

It is thought that Alexander did not only learn of Aristotle moral philosophy and humanity, but also [that] he heard of him [something of those more abstruse and profound theories which these philosophers, by the very names they gave them, professed to reserve for oral communication to the initiated], or else [those which] are kept from common knowledge: which sciences they did not commonly teach. [For when Alexander was in Asia], hearing that Aristotle had put out certain books of that matter, he wrote [to him, using very plain language to him in behalf of philosophy, the following letter]:

> "Alexander unto Aristotle, greeting: Thou hast not
> done well to put forth [your books of oral doctrine]:
> for wherein shall we excel other[s], if those things
> which thou hast secretly taught us, be made
> common to all? I do [wish] thee to understand that
> I had rather excel others in excellency of knowledge,
> than in greatness of power. Farewell."

Whereunto Aristotle, to pacify this his **ambitious humour**, wrote unto him again that these books were [both] **published, and not published**. For to say truly, [his books on metaphysics are written in a style which makes them useless for ordinary teaching, and instructive only in the way of **memoranda**, for those who have already been conversant in that sort of learning].

It seemeth also that it was Aristotle above all other[s], that made Alexander take delight to study physic. For Alexander did not only like the **knowledge of speculation**, but would exercise practice also, and help his friends when they were sick: and made besides certain remedies, and rules to live by: as appeareth by his letters he wrote, that of his own nature he was much **given to his book**, and desired to read much. [Onesicritus informs us that he constantly laid Homer's *Iliads*, according to the copy corrected by Aristotle, called the **"casket copy,"** with his dagger under his pillow, declaring that he esteemed it a perfect portable treasure of all military virtue and knowledge.] And when he was in the high countries of Asia [*later*], where he could not readily come by other books, he wrote unto **Harpalus** to send them to him. Harpalus sent him the histories of Philistus, with divers tragedies of Euripides, Sophocles, and Æschylus: and certain hymns of Telestus and Philoxenus.

Alexander did reverence Aristotle at the first, as his father, and so he termed him: because from his natural father he had life, but from him [Aristotle] the knowledge to live. But afterwards he suspected him somewhat, yet he did him no hurt, neither was he so friendly to him as he had been: whereby men perceived that he did not bear him the goodwill he was wont to do. This notwithstanding, he left not that zeal and desire he had to the study of philosophy, which he had learned from his youth, and still continued.

[*short omission*]

Part Two

When King Philip made war with the Byzantines, Alexander, being but sixteen years old, was left [as] his lieutenant in Macedon, with the custody and charge of his great seal. [Not to sit idle, he] subdued the Medarians which had rebelled against him; and having won their city by assault, he drove out the barbarous people, and made a colony of it of sundry nations, and called it Alexandropolis, to say, "the city of Alexander."

He was with his father at the Battle of Chaeronea against the Grecians, where it was reported that it was he that gave charge first of all upon the holy band of the Thebans. Furthermore, there was an old oak seen in my time, which the countrymen commonly call Alexander's Oak, because his tent or pavilion was fastened to it. [And not far off are to be seen the graves of the Macedonians who fell in that battle.]

For these causes, his father Philip loved him very dearly, and was glad to hear the Macedonians call Alexander king, and himself their captain [*Dryden: general*]. Howbeit the troubles that fell out in his court afterwards, by reason of Philip's new marriages and loves, bred great quarrel and strife amongst the women: for the mischief of dissension and jealousy of women doth separate the hearts of kings one from another. The chiefest cause was the sharpness of **Olympias**, who, being a jealous woman, fretting, and of a revenging mind, did incense Alexander against his father.

[*Omission: events and intrigue involving King Philip, his new second wife* **Cleopatra**, *his other son* **Arrhidaeus**, *and a proposed royal wedding between Arrhidaeus and a Carian princess. When Alexander became involved in this tangle, Philip punished him by banishing several of his friends.*]

Shortly after, **Pausanias**, [*having a personal grudge against Philip*], watched [for] his opportunity and murdered him. Of this murder, most men accused Queen Olympias, who (as it is reported) **allured** this young man, having just cause of anger, to kill him. [There was some sort of suspicion attached even to Alexander himself. [*short omission*] However, he took care to find out and punish the accomplices of the conspiracy severely; and was very angry with Olympias for treating Cleopatra inhumanely in his absence.]

Narration and Discussion

How did Philip recognize and encourage his son's special gifts?

How was Alexander able to accomplish so much before the age of twenty? (You may want to look up 1 Timothy 4:12.)

For older students: If you have read *The Iliad*, do you agree with Alexander's wholehearted admiration of that book? Do you have a book that has become your lifelong guide?

Lesson Three

Introduction

How should a young, ambitious king make the right impression on his country's friends and enemies? In Part One of this lesson, Alexander made a violent choice, but later thought he might have gone too far.

Part Two is a short and much lighter story which should provoke some discussion about material needs and desires.

Vocabulary

barbarous: see introductory notes

insolency: unfriendly attitude, rudeness

magnanimity: this usually means generosity of spirit; but here it means acting unwaveringly. Plutarch adds the phrase "to make them know he was a man."

truckle: bow down

Thebans: those of the Greek city of Thebes

Then did Alexander leave the Macedonians…: He allowed his soldiers to attack without restraint.

make a sally: rush out to attack

an attempt to gratify the hostility of his confederates: his excuse was that he needed to please his allies (and gain their confidence)

those that had dissuaded…: those who had attempted to end the rebellion

Thracian: from the region of Thrace

mien and gait: manner and way of walking

feast of their Mysteries: a time of religious observance

succour: help

clemency: grace, forgiveness

imputed: blamed

in his wine: when he was drunk

within the straits of Peloponnesus: at the city of Corinth

familiars: close friends

what you list: what you wish

People

Demosthenes: an orator in Athens who had spoken against Philip's aggression (see Plutarch's *Life of Demosthenes*)

Philotas and **Antipater:** see introductory notes

Bacchus: the Greek god of wine

Diogenes of Sinope: a founder of Cynic philosophy (forerunner of Stoicism)

Historic Occasions

September, 335 B.C.: Fall of Thebes

On the Map

Alexander's army marched south to Thebes and Corinth.

Reading

Part One

So he came to be king of Macedon at twenty years of age, and found his realm greatly envied and hated of dangerous enemies, and every way full of danger. For the **barbarous** nations that were near neighbours unto Macedon [were impatient of being governed by any but their own native princes]. Neither had Philip time enough to bridle and pacify Greece, which he had conquered by force of arms: but having a little altered the governments, [he] had through his **insolency** left them all in great trouble and ready to rebel, for that they had not long been acquainted to obey.

Thereupon Alexander's council of Macedon, being afraid of the troublesome time, were of opinion that Alexander should utterly forsake the affairs of Greece, and not to follow them with extremity, but that he should seek to win the barbarous people by gentle means, that had rebelled against him, and wisely to remedy these new stirs. [But he rejected this counsel as weak and timorous, and looked upon it to be more prudent to secure himself by resolution and **magnanimity** than by seeming to **truckle** to any, to encourage all to trample on him.]

Thereupon, he straight quenched all the rebellion of the barbarous people, invading them suddenly with his army, by the river Danube, where in a great battle he overthrew Syrmus, king of the Triballians. Furthermore, having intelligence that the **Thebans** [had] revolted, and that the Athenians also were confederate with them: to make them know that he was a man, he marched with his army towards the strait of Thermopiles [*the pass of Thermopylae*], saying that [to **Demosthenes**, who had called him "a child" while he was in Illyria and in the country of the Triballians, and "a youth" when he was in Thessaly, he would appear "a man" before the walls of Athens.]

When he came with his army unto the gates of Thebes, he was willing to give [those] of the city occasion to repent them[selves]: and therefore demanded [only] Phoenix and Prothytes, authors of the rebellion. Furthermore, he proclaimed, by trumpet, pardon and safety unto all them that would yield unto him.

The Thebans, on the other side, demanded of him **Philotas** and **Antipater,** two of his chiefest servants, and made the crier proclaim in the city that all such as would defend the liberty of Greece should join with them. **Then did Alexander leave the Macedonians at liberty to make war with all cruelty.** Then the Thebans fought with greater courage and desire than they were able, considering that their enemies were many against one. And on the other side also, when the garrison of the Macedonians, which were within the [citadel], **made a sally** upon them and gave them charge in the rearward: then they, being environed of all sides, were slain in manner every one of them, their city taken, destroyed, and razed even to the hard ground. This he did, specially to make all the rest of the people of Greece afraid by example of this great calamity and misery of the Thebans, to the end [that] none of them should dare from thenceforth once to rise against him.

He would cloak this cruelty of his under [**an attempt to gratify the hostility of his confederates**]. Notwithstanding, excepting the priests, and the religious, and all such as were friends unto any of the lords of Macedon, all the friends and kinsmen of the poet Pindarus, and all **those that had dissuaded them which were the rebels**: he sold all the rest of the city of Thebes for slaves, which amounted to the number of thirty thousand persons, besides them that were slain at the battle, which were six thousand more.

[Among the other calamities that befell the city, it happened that some **Thracian** soldiers, having broken into the house of a matron of high character and repute named Timoclea; their captain [after otherwise abusing her] asked her if she knew of any money concealed; to which she readily answered she did, and bade him follow her into a garden, where she showed him a well into which, she told him, upon the taking of the city, she had thrown what she had of most value. The greedy Thracian presently stooping down to view the place where he thought the treasure lay, she came behind him and pushed him into the well, and then flung great stones in upon him, till she had killed him. After which, when the solders led her away bound to Alexander, her very **mien and gait** showed her to be a woman of dignity, and of a mind no less elevated, not betraying the least sign of fear or astonishment. And when the king asked her who she was, "I am," said she, "the sister of Theagenes, who fought in the Battle of Chaeronea with your father Philip and fell there in command for the liberty of Greece." Alexander was so surprised, both at what she had done and what she said, that he could not choose but give her and her children their freedom to go whither they pleased.]

He made league also with the Athenians, though they were very sorry for their miserable fortune. For the day of the solemn **feast of their Mysteries** being come, they left it off, mourning for the

Thebans: courteously entertaining all those that, flying from Thebes, came to them for **succour**. But whether it was, [like the lion], that his anger was past him; or by cause that after so great an example of cruelty, he would shew a singular **clemency** again: he did not only pardon the Athenians of all faults committed, but did also counsel them to look wisely to their doings, for their city one day should command all Greece, if he chanced to die.

Men report that certainly he oftentimes repented him that he had dealt so cruelly with the Thebans, and the grief he took upon it was cause that he afterwards shewed himself more merciful unto divers others. [He **imputed** also the murder of Clitus, which he committed **in his wine (Lesson Seventeen)**, and the unwillingness of the Macedonians to follow him against the Indians (**Lesson Twenty**), by which his enterprise and glory was left imperfect, to the wrath and vengeance of **Bacchus,** the protector of Thebes. And it was observed that whatsoever any Theban, who had the good fortune to survive this victory, asked of him, he was sure to grant without the least difficulty.]

Part Two

Then the Grecians having assembled a general council of all the states of Greece **within the straits of Peloponnesus**: there it was determined that they would make war with the Persians. Whereupon they chose Alexander general for all Greece.

Then divers men coming to visit Alexander, as well [as] philosophers [and] governors of states, to congratulate with him for his election, he looked that **Diogenes of Sinope** (who dwelt at Corinth) would likewise come as the rest had done: but when he saw he made no reckoning of him, and that he kept still in the suburbs of Corinth, at a place called [the] Cranium, he went himself unto him, and found him laid all along in the sun.

When Diogenes saw so many coming towards him, he sat up a little, and looked full upon Alexander. Alexander courteously spake unto him, and asked him if he lacked anything. "Yea," said he, "that I do: that thou stand out of my sun a little."

Alexander was so well pleased with this answer, and marvelled so much at the great boldness of this man, to see how small account he made of him: that when he went his way from him, Alexander's

familiars laughing at Diogenes and mocking him, he told them, "Masters, say **what you list**, truly if I were not Alexander, I would be Diogenes."

[*omitted material between lessons*]

Narration and Discussion

Alexander was advised to introduce himself as a friendly, gentle ruler of the cities his father had conquered. Why did he reject this advice?

Why did Alexander say that he would choose to be Diogenes? Do you agree?

Older students: Part One of this lesson raises many questions about military aggression, including the treatment of civilians during wars. Could Alexander's destruction of Thebes be justified? If so, why did he later regret his actions?

Lesson Four

Introduction

In this lesson, Alexander fought successfully to cross the Granicus River and enter Persian territory. King Darius was not there himself; perhaps he thought it would be an easy matter for his troops (made up largely of mercenary soldiers) to push the Macedonians back.

Vocabulary

Delphi, to consult Apollo: the temple at Delphi contained the Oracle, believed to be a source of supernatural guidance. The prophecies were spoken through a woman called **"the priestess"** or "the nun."

prodigies: supernatural occurrences

the custom of some haven: the revenue (income) from a harbour

liberality: generosity

Alexander

to tarry Alexander...: to keep the Macedonians from crossing the river

fight pell-mell: fight quickly and without much strategy

partisan: spear

phalanx: the classic Macedonian battle formation

the mercenary Greeks: hired soldiers who were fighting for Persia

People

Aristander: a soothsayer

Perdiccas, Darius: see introductory notes

Achilles, Paris: characters in Homer's *Iliad*

Clitus (Cleitus): "Clitus the Black" saved Alexander's life in this battle, but was killed by him six years later during a drunken quarrel

Historic Occasions

June, 334 B.C.: Battle of the **Granicus River**

334 B.C.: The city of Sardis surrendered to Alexander

On the Map

After visiting Delphi, Alexander returned to Macedonia, gathered his forces, and headed east and then south, around the Aegean Sea, crossing the **Strait of Hellespont** (the boundary between Europe and Asia, also called the Bosphorus); and finally arriving at the ancient site of Troy. The Granicus River was east of Troy.

Reading

Part One

[Then he went to **Delphi, to consult Apollo** concerning the success of the war he had undertaken; and happening to come on one of the forbidden days, when it was esteemed improper to give any answer from the oracle, he sent messengers to desire **the priestess** to do her office; and when she refused, on the plea of a law to the contrary, he went up himself, and began to draw her by force into the temple, until tired and overcome with his importunity: "My son," said she, "thou art invincible." Alexander taking hold of what she spoke, declared he had received such an answer as he wished for, and that it was needless to consult the god any further.

Among other **prodigies** that attended the departure of his army, the image of Orpheus at Libethra, made of cypress-wood, was seen to sweat in great abundance, to the discouragement of many. But **Aristander** told him that, far from presaging any ill to him, it signified he should perform acts so important and glorious as would make the poets and musicians of future ages labour and sweat to describe and celebrate them.]

Then, for his army which he led with him, they that do set down the least number, say that they were thirty thousand footmen, and five thousand horsemen: and they that say more, do write four and thirty thousand footmen, and four thousand horsemen. Aristobulus writeth that Alexander had no more but three score and ten talents to pay his soldiers with: and Duris writeth that he had no more provision of victuals than for thirty days only. And Onesicritus sayeth, moreover, that he did owe two hundred talents.

Now, notwithstanding that he began this war with so small ability to maintain it, he would never take ship before he understood the state of his friends, to know what ability they had to go with him, and before he had given unto some, lands, and unto other[s], a town, and to others again, **the custom of some haven**. Thus, by his bounty having in manner spent almost the revenues of the crown of Macedon, **Perdiccas** asked him: "My lord, what will you keep for yourself?" "Hope," said he. "Then," quoth Perdiccas again, "we will also have some part, since we go with you," and so [he] refused the revenue which the king had given him for his pension. Many others did also the like. But such as were contented to take his **liberality**, or would ask him anything, he gave them very frankly, and in such liberality [he] spent all the revenue he had.

With this desire and determination, he went on to the **Strait of**

Alexander

Hellespont, and going to the city of Ilium [Dryden: *Troy*], he did sacrifice unto Diana [Dryden: *Minerva*], and made funeral effusions unto the demi-gods (to wit, unto the princes which died in the war of Troy, whose bodies were buried there) and specially unto **Achilles**, whose grave he anointed with oil, and ran naked round about it with his familiars, according to the ancient custom of funerals. Then he covered it with nosegays and flowers, saying that Achilles was happy, who while he lived had a faithful friend, and after his death an excellent herald to sing his praise. When he had done, and went up and down the city to see all the monuments and notable things, there [some]one asked him if he would [like to] see **Paris'** harp. He answered again, he would [prefer to] see Achilles' harp, who played and sang upon it all the famous acts done by valiant men in former times.

Part Two

In the meantime, **Darius**, king of Persia, having levied a great army, sent his captains and lieutenants **to tarry Alexander** at the **Granicus River**. There was Alexander to fight of necessity, [it] being the only bar to stop his entry into Asia. Moreover, [his generals] were afraid of the depth of this river, and of the height of the bank on the other side, which was very high and steep, and could not be won without fighting. And some said also, that he should have special care of the ancient regard of the month: because the kings of Macedon did never use to put their army into the field in the month of *Dason* [*Daesius*], which is June. "For that," said Alexander, "we will remedy soon: let them call it the second month, *Artemisium*, which is May." Furthermore, Parmenio was of opinion that he should not meddle the first day, because it was very late. Alexander made answer again, that [the] Hellespont would blush for shame if he were now afraid to pass over the river, since he had already come over an arm of the sea.

Thereupon he himself first entered the river with thirteen [troops] of horsemen, and marched forwards against an infinite number of arrows which the enemies shot at him as he was coming up the other bank, which was very high and steep, and worst of all, full of armed men and horsemen of the enemies: which stayed to receive him in battle array, thrusting his men down into the river, which was very deep, and ran so swift that it almost carried them down the stream:

insomuch that men thought him more rash than wise, to lead his men with such danger. [However, he persisted obstinately to gain the passage, and at last with much ado he] recovered the other side, specially because the earth slid away, by reason of the mud.

So when he was [crossed] over, he was driven to **fight pell-mell** one upon another, because his enemies did set upon the first that were passed over, before they could put themselves into battle array, with great cries, keeping their horses very close together, and fought first with their darts, and afterwards came to the sword when their darts were broken. Then many of them set upon him alone, for he was easily to be known above the rest by his shield and the hinder part of his helmet, about the which there hung, from the one side to the other, a marvellous fair white plume. Alexander had a blow with a dart on his thigh, but it hurt him not.

Part Three

Thereupon Roesaces and Spithridates, two chief captains of the Persians, setting upon Alexander at once: he left the one, and riding straight to Roesaces, who was excellently armed, he gave him such a blow with his lance that he broke it in his hand, and straight drew out his sword. But so soon as they two had closed together, Spithridates coming at the side of him, raised himself upon his stirrups and gave Alexander with all his might such a blow of his head with a battleaxe, that he cut [off] the crest of his helmet, and one of the sides of his plume, and made such a gash that the edge of his battleaxe touched the very hair of his head. And as he was lifting up his hand to strike Alexander again, great **Clitus**, preventing him, thrust him through with a **partisan**; and at the very same instant, Roesaces also fell dead from his horse with a wound which Alexander gave him with his sword.

Now whilst the horsemen fought with such fury, [the Macedonian **phalanx** passed the river, and the foot [soldiers] on each side advanced to fight. But the enemy hardly sustaining the first onset soon gave ground and fled, all but **the mercenary Greeks**, who] drew together upon a hill, and craved mercy of Alexander. But Alexander setting upon them, more of will than discretion, had his horse killed under him, being thrust through the flank with a sword. This was not Bucephalus, but another horse he had.

All his men that were slain or hurt at this battle were hurt [*because they were*] valiantly fighting against desperate men. It is reported that there were slain, at this first battle, twenty thousand footmen of these barbarous people, and two thousand five hundred horsemen. Of Alexander's side, Aristobulus writeth that there were slain four and thirty men in all, of the which twelve of them were footmen. Alexander, to honour their valiantness, caused every one of their images to be made in brass by Lysippus. And because he would make the Grecians partakers of this victory, he sent unto the Athenians three hundred [Persian] targets, which he had won at the battle, and [upon the rest] he put this honourable inscription: "Alexander the son of Philip, and the Grecians, excepting the Lacedaemonians, have won this spoil upon the barbarous Asians."

[All the plate and purple garments, and other things of the same kind that he took from the Persians (except a very small quantity which he reserved for himself), he sent as a present to his mother.]

Narration and Discussion

Why did Alexander take the words of the irritated priestess as a prophecy?

If you could see and touch some artifact from history or from literature), what would you choose?

Creative narration: In a journal entry, or a letter to someone at home, describe the crossing of the Granicus.

Lesson Five

Introduction

After the initial victory at the Battle of Granicus, the Macedonians seemed to have gained a great deal more respect from the Persian cities they passed through. Alexander and Darius both expected that they would soon fight face to face, but this was delayed by Alexander's serious illness in Cilicia.

Vocabulary

the empire of the barbarous people: the Persian empire

by the Grecians: in this case, "Grecians" refers to the Macedonians

Cilicia: a region within the Persian empire, part of present-day Turkey

clear: conquer

the knot: the Gordian Knot (see note before the reading)

levied: assembled

Susa: an important city of Persia

extreme pains and travail: exhaustion, overwork

miscarried: failed, or, in this case, died

People

Philip [the] Acarnanian: Alexander's personal physician

Historic Occasions

April-July, 333 B.C.: Alexander's visit to Gordium

September, 333 B.C.: Alexander arrived in Cilicia and became ill

On the Map

In Part One, the Macedonians' route after Granicus was south to Sardis, and then west to the Mediterranean, where they followed the coast around what is now southern Turkey, to the city of Phaselis.

In Part Two, they seem to have gone north (Gordium is more than halfway up to the Black Sea), and then looped around south again (Cilicia was in the Mediterranean region).

Alexander

What was the Gordian Knot?

In Phrygia, once upon a time, it was decided that the next man to enter the city would become king. A farmer named Gordias came along driving an ox-cart, was therefore named king, and his now-unneeded cart was left there, tied up with an intricate knot. (Interestingly, Gordias is supposed to have been from Macedonia.) A legend grew up that the one who undid the knot would rule Asia, and many would-be rulers tried but failed. Most tellers of the story say that Alexander simply cut the knot; but Plutarch offers an alternative version, saying that it was possible to undo the knot by removing the linchpin (a fastener) from the cart wheel.

"Cutting a Gordian knot" refers to a bold or unexpected solution to a difficult problem. But the famous preacher Charles Haddon Spurgeon, in a sermon titled "God's Providence," did not approve of Alexander's method, or (perhaps more) of his arrogance. He said, "God has many Gordian knots which wicked men may cut and which righteous men may try to unravel, but which God alone can untie."

Reading

Part One

This first victory brought such a sudden change amongst the barbarous people in Alexander's behalf, that the city [it]self of Sardis, the chief city of **the empire of the barbarous people**, or at the least through all the low countries and coasts upon the sea, they yielded straight unto him, [excepting] the cities of Halicarnassus and Miletus, which did still resist him: howbeit at length he took them by force.

When he had also conquered all thereabouts, he stood in doubt afterwards [about what were best to do]. Sometime[s] he had a marvellous desire wholly to follow Darius, wheresoever he were, and to venture all at a battle. Another time again, he thought it better first to occupy himself in conquering of these low countries, and to make himself strong with the money and riches he should find among them, that he might afterwards be the better able to follow him.

[While he was thus deliberating what to do, it happened that a spring of water near the city of Xanthus in Lycia, of its own accord, swelled over its banks, and threw up a copper plate, upon the margin of which was engraven in ancient characters, that the time would come] when the kingdom of the Persians should be destroyed **by the Grecians**. This did further so encourage Alexander that he made haste to **clear** all the sea coast, even as far as **Cilicia** and Phoenicia. But the wonderful good success he had, running alongst all the coast of Pamphilia, gave divers historiographers occasion to set forth his doings with admiration, saying that it was one of the wonders of the world that the fury of the sea, which unto all other was extreme[ly] rough, and many times would swell over the tops of the high rocks upon the cliffs, fell calm unto him.

[*short omission for length*]

Part Two

[Then he subdued the Pisidians who made head against him, and conquered the Phrygians, at whose chief city, **Gordium**, which is said to be the seat of the ancient Midas, he saw the famous chariot fastened with cords made of the rind of the cornel-tree, which whosoever should untie, the inhabitants had a tradition that for him was reserved the empire of the world. Most authors tell the story that Alexander finding himself unable to untie **the knot**, the ends of which were secretly twisted round and folded up within it, cut it asunder with his sword. But Aristobulus tells us it was easy for him to undo it, by only pulling the pin out of the pole to which the yoke was tied, and afterwards drawing off the yoke itself from below.]

Departing thence, he conquered the Paphlagonians and Cappadocians. [Hearing of] the death of Memnon, that was Darius' general of his army by sea, and in whom was all their hope to trouble and withstand Alexander: whereupon he was the bolder to go on with his determination to lead his army into the high countries of Asia.

Part Three

Then did King Darius himself come against Alexander, having **levied** a great power at **Susa** of six hundred thousand fighting men; trusting to that multitude, and also to a dream, the which his wizards had expounded rather to flatter him than to tell him truly. Darius dreamed that he saw all the army of the Macedonians [all on fire], and Alexander serving of him in the same attire that he himself wore when he was [courier] unto the late king his predecessor; and that when he came into the temple of Belus, he [Alexander] suddenly vanished from him. By this dream it plainly appeared that the gods did signify unto him that the Macedonians should have noble success in their doings, and that [as he, from a courier's place, had risen to the throne, so Alexander should come to be master of Asia, and not long surviving his conquests, conclude his life with glory].

This furthermore made him bold also, when he saw that Alexander remained a good while in **Cilicia**, supposing it had been for that he was afraid of him. Howbeit it was by reason of a sickness he (Alexander) had, the which some say he got by **extreme pains and travail**, and others also, because he washed himself in the river of Cydnus, which was cold as ice. Howsoever it came, there was none of the other physicians that durst undertake to cure him, thinking his disease uncurable, and no medicines to prevail that they could give him, and fearing also that the Macedonians would lay it to their charge if Alexander **miscarried**.

But **Philip [the] Acarnanian**, considering his master was very ill, and bearing himself of his love and goodwill towards him, thought he should not do that [which] became him, if he did not prove (seeing him in extremity and danger of life) the utmost remedies of physic, what danger soever he put himself into: and therefore took upon him to minister physic unto Alexander, and persuaded him to drink it boldly if he would quickly be whole, and go to the wars.

In the meantime, Parmenio wrote him (Alexander) a letter from the camp, advertising him that he should beware of Philip his physician, for [he said that Philip] was bribed and corrupted by Darius, with large promises of great riches that he would give him, [along] with his daughter in marriage, to kill his master.

Alexander when he had read this letter, laid it under his bed's head, and made none of his nearest familiars acquainted therewith. When the hour came that he should take his medicine, Philip came into his chamber, with [some] of the king's familiars, and brought a cup in his hand with the potion he should drink. Alexander then gave him the letter, and withal, cheerfully took the cup of him, shewing no manner of fear or mistrust of anything. It was a wonderful thing and worth the sight, how one reading the letter, and the other drinking the medicine both at one instant, they looked one upon another, howbeit not both with like cheerful countenance.

For Alexander looked merrily upon him, plainly shewing the trust he had in his physician Philip, and how much he loved him: and the physician also beheld Alexander, like a man perplexed and amazed, to be so falsely accused, and straight lift[ed] up his hands to heaven, calling the gods to witness that he was innocent, and then came to Alexander's bedside, and prayed him to be of good cheer, and boldly to do as he would advise him.

The medicine, beginning to work, overcame the disease, and drove, for the time, to the lowest parts of his body, all his natural strength and powers: insomuch as his speech failed him, and he fell into such a weakness, and almost swooning, that his pulse did scant beat, and his senses were well near taken from him. But that being past, Philip in (a) few days recovered him again.

Now, when Alexander had gotten some strength, he showed himself openly unto the Macedonians: for they would not be pacified, nor persuaded of his health, until they had seen him.

Narration and Discussion

Why did Alexander have so much success in conquering these regions of the Persian empire? To what did he give the credit?

Was Alexander's illness a Gordian knot for his physician?

Creative narration: The "wizards" (or "wise men") of Darius used his dream about Alexander to boost his confidence, by twisting its meaning. Plutarch's description of the dream, however, does not sound very affirming. How might it have been re-interpreted to sound more positive? This is a scene that could be written or acted out.

Creative narration: Both the cutting of the Gordian knot and the scene between Alexander and Philip would lend themselves to drama, art, or creative writing. (Could they be "modernized?")

Alexander

Lesson Six

Introduction

Plutarch sets the scene for the Battle of Issus, stating that the odds were against the Macedonians from the beginning: they were outnumbered and at a geographical disadvantage. Somehow, through good leadership and perhaps good luck, the Macedonians won an unexpected victory. King Darius escaped, leaving everything behind including his relatives and his bathtub.

Vocabulary

Cilician Gates: a pass through the mountains into that region

tarry: remain

his horse: the Macedonian cavalry

sumptuous: rich, luxurious.

People

Amyntas: Alexander had an officer named Amyntas, but this is someone else with the same name.

Antipater: see introductory notes

Historic Occasions

November, 333 B.C.: Battle of Issus

On the Map

Issus is in the large gulf at the northeastern corner of the Mediterranean, between Antioch and Tarsus.

Reading

In King Darius' camp, there was one **Amyntas**, a Macedonian, and banished out of his country, who knew Alexander's disposition very well. He, finding that Darius meant to meet with Alexander within the straits and valleys of the mountains, besought him to **tarry** rather where he was, [there] being a plain open country round about him, considering that he had a great host of men to fight with a few enemies, and that it was most for his advantage to meet with him in the open field. [Darius, instead of taking his counsel, told him he was afraid the enemy would endeavour to run away, and so Alexander would escape out of his hands.] Amyntas replied, "For that, O King, I pray you fear not: for I warrant you upon my life he will come to you, yea and is now onwards on his way coming towards you." All these persuasions of Amyntas could not turn Darius from making his camp to march towards Cilicia.

At the same time also, Alexander went towards Syria to meet with him. But it chanced one night, that the one of them missed of the other, and when day was come, they both returned back again.

Alexander, being glad of this hap, [made] haste to meet with his enemy within the straits. [Darius attempted to recover his former ground and draw his army out of so disadvantageous a place. For now, he began to perceive his error in engaging himself too far in a country in which the sea, the mountains, and the river Pinarus running through the midst of it, would necessitate him to divide his forces, render **his horse** almost unserviceable, and only cover and support the weakness of the enemy.] But now, as fortune gave Alexander the field as he would wish it to fight for his advantage, so could he tell excellently well how to set his men in battle array to win the victory. [For being much inferior in numbers, so far from allowing himself to be outflanked], he did put out the right wing of his battle a great deal further than he did his left wing; and fighting himself in the left wing in the foremost ranks, he made all the barbarous people flee that stood before him: howbeit, he was hurt on his thigh with a blow of a sword. Chares writeth that Darius himself did hurt him, and that they fought together man to man. Notwithstanding, Alexander himself, writing of this battle unto **Antipater**, sayeth that indeed he was hurt on the thigh with a sword, howbeit it did put him in no danger: but he writeth not that Darius did hurt him.

Thus, having won a famous victory, and slain above a hundred and ten thousand of his enemies, he could not yet take Darius, because he fled, having still four or five furlongs' [ad]vantage before him: howbeit he [Alexander] took his chariot of battle wherein he fought, and his bow also. Then he [Alexander] returned from the chase, and found the Macedonians sacking and spoiling all the rest of the camp of the barbarous people, where there was infinite riches (although they had left the most part of their carriage behind them in the city of Damascus, to come lighter to the battle); but [they] yet reserved for himself all King Darius' tent, which was full of a great number of rich moveables, and of gold and silver. So, when he was come to the camp, putting off his armour, he entered into the bath and said, "Come on, let us go and wash off the sweat of the battle in Darius' own bath."

"Nay," replied one of his familiars again, "in Alexander's bath; for the goods of the vanquished are rightly the vanquisher's." When he came into the bath, and saw the basins and ewers, the boxes, and vials for perfumes, all of clean gold, excellently wrought, all the chamber perfumed passing sweetly, that it was like a paradise; then going out of his bath, and coming into his tent, seeing it so stately and large, his bed, the table, and supper, and all ready in such **sumptuous** sort, that it was wonderful, he turned him unto his familiars and said: "This was a king indeed, was he not, think ye?" [Dryden: *"This, it seems, is royalty."*]

Narration and Discussion

Why did Darius not take the advice of Amyntas, and fight in the open country where he was? Explain Amyntas' response.

What does this passage show about the character and leadership of Alexander?

Creative narration: You are a reporter on the scene after the Battle of Issus. Try to interview a variety of onlookers and participants. (This could be acted or written.) Another possibility: make a "Most Wanted" poster for King Darius, giving pertinent details.

The Plutarch Project

Lesson Seven

Introduction

This lesson concludes the Battle of Issus, but it deals mainly with the generous and gallant aspects of Alexander's character.

Vocabulary

clemency: grace, generosity

suffered: allowed

pensions: financial allowances

usage: treatment

preceptor, governor: tutor and personal trainer

fine knacks or conceits: self-indulgent luxuries

bibber: drinker

curious: careful; **he was nothing curious** means he cared nothing

a great advantage to ride him: an opportunity to mock him

People

Princess Ada: Ada of Caria has an interesting history as a ruler. When Alexander entered her region of Caria (in present-day Turkey), Ada surrendered the fort she was holding, and in return he gave her command of the Siege of Halicarnassus.

Reading

As he was ready to go to his supper, word was brought [to] him that they were bringing unto him, amongst other ladies taken prisoners, King Darius' mother and his wife, and two of his daughters unmarried: who, having seen his chariot and bow, burst out into lamentable cries, and violent beating of themselves, thinking Darius had been slain. Alexander paused a good while and gave no answer, pitying more their misfortune than rejoicing at his own good hap. Then he presently sent one Leonatus unto them, to let them understand that Darius was alive, and that they should not need to be afraid of Alexander, for he did not fight with Darius, but for his kingdom only; and as for them, that they should have at his hands all that they had of Darius before, when he had his whole kingdom in his hands.

As these words pleased the captive ladies, so the deeds that followed made them find his **clemency** to be no less. For first he **suffered** them to bury as many of the Persian lords as they would, even of them that had been slain in the battle, and to take as much silks of the spoils, jewels, and ornaments, as they thought good to honour their funerals with; and also [he] did lessen no part of their honour, nor of the number of their officers and servants, nor of any jot of their estate which they had before, but did allow them also greater **pensions** than they had before. [But the noblest and most royal part of their **usage** was that he treated these illustrious prisoners according to their virtue and character, not suffering them to hear, or receive, or so much as to apprehend anything that was unbecoming. So that they seemed rather lodged in some temple, or some holy virgin chambers, where they enjoyed their privacy sacred and uninterrupted, than in the camp of an enemy.]

[*omission: examples of Alexander's chastity*]

He was also no greedy gut, but temperate in eating, as he showed by many proofs: but chiefly in [what] he said unto **Princess Ada**, whom he adopted for his mother, and [afterwards created] queen of Caria. [For when she, out of kindness, sent him every day many curious dishes and sweetmeats, and would have furnished him with some cooks and pastry-men, who were thought to have great skills, he told her he wanted none of them, his **preceptor**, Leonidas, having already given him the best, which were a night march to prepare for breakfast, and a moderate breakfast to create an appetite for supper.] "And my **governor**," said he, "would oftentimes open the chests where my bedding and apparel lay, to see if my mother had put any **fine knacks or conceits** among them."

Furthermore, he was less given to wine than men would have judged. For he was thought to be a greater **bibber** than he was, because he sat long at the board, rather to talk than [to] drink, [and over every cup hold a long conversation. For when his affairs called upon him, he would not be detained as other generals often were either by wine, or sleep, nuptial solemnities, spectacles, or any other diversion whatsoever; a convincing argument of which is, that in the short time he lived, he accomplished so many and so great actions.]

When he had leisure, after he was up in the morning, first of all he would do sacrifice to the gods, and then would go to dinner, passing away all the rest of the day in hunting, writing something, taking up some quarrel between soldiers, or else in studying. If he went [on] any journey of no hasty business, he would exercise himself by the way as he went, shooting in his bow, or learning to get up or out of his chariot suddenly, as it ran. Oftentimes also for his pastime he would hunt the fox or catch birds, as appeareth in his book of remembrances for every day. Then when he came to his lodging, he would enter into his bath, and rub and anoint himself, and would ask his [bakers and chief cooks] if his supper were ready. He would ever sup late, and [he] was very **curious** to see that every man at his board were alike served, and [he] would sit long at the table, because he ever loved to talk, as we have told you before. Otherwise he was as noble a prince and gracious to wait upon, and as pleasant as any king that ever was.

For he lacked no grace nor comeliness to adorn a prince, saving that he would be something overbusy in glorying in his own deeds, much like unto a bragging soldier [which gave his flatterers **a great advantage to ride him**, and made his better friends uneasy]. And this was many times the destruction of honest men about him, [who] would neither praise him in his presence, hating the flatterers, nor yet [dare] say less of the praises which they gave him. For of the first they were ashamed, and by the second they fell in danger.

After supper, he would wash himself again, and sleep until noon the next day following, and oftentimes all day long.

For himself, **he was nothing curious** of dainty dishes: for when any did send him rare fruits, or fish, from the countries near the seaside, he would send them abroad unto his friends, and seldom keep anything for himself. His table notwithstanding was always very honourably served, and [he] did still increase his fare, as he did enlarge his conquests: till it came to the sum of ten thousand drachmas a day. But there he stayed, and would not exceed that sum, and moreover commanded all men that would feast him, that they should not spend above that sum.

Narration and Discussion

How did Alexander treat the female relatives of King Darius? What does this show about his character?

In what ways did Alexander show moderation in his personal life? How did those habits allow him to get a lot done?

Lesson Eight

Introduction

Alexander never seemed to stop moving and conquering. His army bulldozed southward through many ancient strongholds, eventually taking even the stubborn city of Tyre.

Vocabulary

barbarous: in this case, the luxurious Persian lifestyle

necessary to assure himself of the seacoast: he needed to take control of the ports along the coast of the Mediterranean

bulwarks and divers engines of battery: war machines and weapons

Mount Antilibanus: mountains between Syria and Lebanon

benighted: forced to stop for the night

firebrand: torch, or blazing stick of wood from the fire

entrails: innards

prognosticate: prophesy

frankincense, myrrh: aromatic (fragrant) gum resins, burned as incense

People

Lysimachus, Leonidas: see introductory notes

Phoenix, Achilles' guardian: Phoenix went with Achilles to the Trojan war, in Homer's *Iliad*

Historic Occasions

332 B.C.: Alexander conquered Tyre in Phoenicia, then Syria

On the Map

Alexander followed the eastern coast of the Mediterranean, through Phoenicia, and besieged **Tyre**. The Macedonians then marched through Syria and Palestine (including the city of **Gaza**).

Reading

Part One

After the Battle of Issus (**Lesson Six**), he sent unto the city of Damascus, to take all the gold and silver, the carriage, and all the women and children of the Persians which were left there [of which spoil the Thessalian horsemen had the greatest share]. For therefore did he send them [the Thessalians] thither, because he saw that they had fought valiantly at the day of the battle; and so were the rest of his army also well stored with money. There the Macedonians having tasted first of the gold, silver, women, and **barbarous** life: as dogs by scent do follow the track of beasts, even so were they greedy to follow after the goods of the Persians. [But Alexander, before he proceeded any further, thought it **necessary to assure himself of the seacoast**. Those who governed in Cyprus put that island into his possession, and Phoenicia, [the city of] **Tyre** only excepted, was surrendered to him.] That city he besieged seven months together by land, with great **bulwarks and divers engines of battery,** and by sea, with two

Alexander

hundred galleys.

[*omission for length: Alexander's dreams of Hercules and mythical beasts*]

Continuing this siege, he went to make war with the Arabians that dwell upon [**Mount Antilibanus**, in which he hazarded his life extremely to (save) his master **Lysimachus**, who would needs go along with him, declaring that he was neither "older nor inferior in courage to **Phoenix**," **Achilles' guardian**]. For when they came at the foot of the mountain, they left their horses, and went up afoot: and Alexander was of so courteous a nature, that he would not leave his tutor Lysimachus behind him (who was so weary that he could go no further); but because it was dark night, and for that the enemies were not far from them, he came behind to encourage his tutor, and in manner to carry him. By this means, unwares, he was far from his army with very few men about him, and **benighted** besides: moreover, it was very cold, and the way was very ill.

At the length, perceiving divers fires which the enemies had made, some in one place, and some in another, trusting to his valiantness, having always provided remedy in extremity when the Macedonians were distressed, himself ever putting to his own hand: he ran unto them that had made the fires next him, and killing two of the barbarous people that lay by the fireside, he snatched away a **firebrand**, and ran with it to his own men, who made a great fire. At this the barbarous people were so afraid, that they ran their way as fast as they could. Other[s] also thinking to come and set upon him, he slew them every man, and so lay there that night, himself and his men without danger. Thus Chares reporteth this matter.

Part Two

Now for the **siege of Tyre**, that fell out thus. Alexander caused the most part of his army to take rest, being overharried and wearied with so many battles as they had fought: and sent a few of his men only to give assault unto the city, to keep the Tyrians occupied, that they should take no rest. One day the soothsayer Aristander sacrificing unto the gods, having considered of the signs of the **entrails** of the beasts, did assure them that were present, that the city should be taken by the latter end of the month. Everybody laughed to hear him: for that day was the very last day of the month. Alexander seeing him amazed, as one that could not tell what to say to it, seeking ever to bring those tokens to effect which the soothsayers did **prognosticate**: [he gave orders that they should not count it as the thirtieth, but as the twenty-third of the month]. He made the trumpet sound the alarm, and give a hotter assault to the wall than he had thought to have done before. They fought valiantly on both sides, insomuch as they that were left in the camp could not keep in but must needs run to the assault to help their companions. The Tyrians seeing the assault so hot on every side, their hearts began to fail them, and by this means was the city taken the selfsame day.

[*short omission*]

Part Three

[Alexander] sent great presents of spoils which he won at the sack of **Gaza** unto his mother Olympias, [his stepmother] Cleopatra, and divers others of his friends. Among other things, he sent unto **Leonidas**, his governor, five hundred talents' weight of **frankincense** and a hundred talents' weight of **myrrh**, remembering the hope he put him into when he was a child. For, as Alexander was upon a day sacrificing unto the gods, he took both his hands full of frankincense to cast into the fire, to make a perfume thereof. When Leonidas saw him, he said thus unto him: "When thou hast conquered the country where these sweet things grow, then be liberal of thy perfume: but now, spare that little thou hast at this present." Alexander calling to mind at that time his admonition, wrote unto him in this sort: "We do send thee plenty of frankincense and myrrh, because thou shouldst no more be a [miser] unto the gods."

Narration and Discussion

Alexander's world was full of prophecies, dreams, and sacrifices to gods. At the same time, Alexander's methods of warfare seem to have been extremely practical: war engines, sieges, and, when necessary, stealing fire and stabbing those he believed to be enemies. Does he seem to have put more trust in the supernatural, or in his own strength?

How did Alexander's gift to his old tutor show a sense of humour?

Lesson Nine

Introduction

Alexander marked his time in Egypt first by laying out plans for the city of Alexandria, and then by taking an arduous pilgrimage through the desert to the temple of Jupiter Ammon.

Vocabulary

casket: box, chest

laid up: stored

a great city: Alexandria

these verses: these are lines from Homer's *Odyssey*

being forced by man's hand: it was later joined to the mainland by a "mole" or stone causeway

isthmus: a narrow strip of land

the charge of the building: Alexander remained in Egypt for only a few months and never saw more than the foundations of the city.

dissuade: talk someone out of something

he had power also of time and place: Alexander seemed to have influence over even non-human factors

element: sky, heavens

no mortal man: the priest was not referring to Philip

it went for current: the story went

divine generation: being born of gods

Historic Occasions

331? B.C.: the founding of Alexandria. Some sources give the date as 332, or even 334.

On the Map

The Macedonians made a long, looping journey through the northern part of Egypt (stopping to establish Alexandria on the Mediterranean coast, west of the Nile River delta). This detour was due to Alexander's wish to visit the temple of **Jupiter Ammon**, or Zeus Ammon. Ammon was the Greek name for the Egyptian god Aman; they must have found it fitting, because "ammos" is the Greek word for "sand."

Reading

Part One

[Among the treasures and other booty that was taken from Darius, there was a very precious **casket**, which, being brought to Alexander for a great rarity, he asked those about him what they thought fittest to be **laid up** in it.] Some said one thing, some said another thing: but he said, he would put Homer's *Iliad* into it, as the worthiest thing. This is confirmed by the best historiographers; [and if what those of Alexandria tell us, relying upon the authority of Heraclides, be true], then it appeareth that he did profit himself much by Homer in this journey.

For it is reported that when he had conquered Egypt, he determined to build **a great city**, and to replenish it with a great number of Grecians, and to call it after his name. But as he was about to enclose a certain ground, which he had chosen by the advice of his engineers and workmasters: the night before he had a marvellous dream, that he saw an old man standing before him, full of white hairs, with an honourable presence, [who] coming towards him said **these verses**:

["An island lies, where loud the billows roar,

Pharos, they call it, on the Egyptian shore."]

As soon as he rose the next morning, he went to see this isle of Pharos, which at that time was a little above the mouth of the river Nile, called Canobia; howbeit, it is now joined unto firm land, **being forced by man's hand**. [As soon as he saw the commodious situation of the place, it being a long neck of land, stretching like an **isthmus** between large lagoons and shallow waters on one side and the sea on the other, the latter at the end of it making a spacious harbour, he said, "Homer, besides his other excellences, was a very good architect," and [he] ordered the plan of a city to be drawn out answerable to the place. To do which, for want of chalk, the soil being black, they laid out their lines with flour [Dryden: *meal*], taking in a pretty large compass of ground in a semi-circular figure, and drawing into the inside of the circumference equal straight lines from each end, thus giving it something of the form of a cloak or cape. While he was pleasing himself with his design, on a sudden an infinite number of great birds of several kinds, rising like a black cloud out of the river and the lake, devoured every morsel of the flour that had been used in setting out the lines; at which omen even Alexander himself was troubled.] Notwithstanding, his soothsayers bade him not be discouraged, for they told him it was a sign that he should build a city there, so plentiful of all things, that he should maintain all sorts of people. Then he commanded them unto whom he had given **the charge of the building**, that they should go forward with their work; and he himself, in the meantime, took his journey to go visit the temple of **Jupiter Ammon**.

Part Two

The journey was long, and there were many troubles by the way, but two dangers above all the rest most special. The first, lack of water, because they had to travel many days' journey through a great desert. The second was, the danger of the rising of the south wind by the way, to blow the sand abroad, which was of a wonderful length. And it is reported, that on a time there rose such a tempest in that desert, that blew up whole hills of sand [as it is said to have done when Cambyses led his army that way]. Every man in Alexander's train did know these dangers very well: howbeit it was hard to **dissuade** Alexander from anything which he had a desire unto. For Fortune, favouring him in all his attempts, made him constant and resolute in his determinations: and his noble courage, besides, made him invincible in all things he took in hand, insomuch as he did not only compel his enemies, but **he had power also of time and place**.

In that voyage, instead of these former dangers spoken of, he had many helps, which are supposed were sent him from the gods by the oracles that followed afterwards. For in a certain sort, [*men*] have believed the oracles that were written of him. First of all, the wonderful water and great showers that fell from the **element** did keep him from fear of the first danger, and did quench their thirst, and moistened the dryness of the sand in such sort, that there came a sweet fresh air from it. Furthermore, when the marks were hidden from the guides to shew them the way, and they wandered up and down, they could not tell where: there came crows unto them that did guide them, flying before them: flying fast when they saw them follow them, and stay[ing] for them when they were behind. But Callisthenes writeth a greater wonder than this: that in the nighttime, with the very noise of the crows, they brought them again into the right way [those] which had lost their way.

Thus, Alexander in the end having passed through this wilderness, he came unto the temple he sought for: where the prophet or chief priest saluted him from the god Ammon, as from his father. Then Alexander asked him, if any of the murderers that had killed his father were left alive. The priest answered him, and bade him take heed he did not blaspheme, for his father was **no mortal man**. Then Alexander [*brief omission*] asked him if the murderers that had conspired the death of Philip his father were all punished. After that he asked him, touching his kingdom, if he would grant him to be king over all the world. The god answered him by the mouth of his prophet, he should: and that the death of Philip was fully revenged. Then did Alexander offer great presents unto the god, and [he] gave [much] money to the priests and ministers of the temple. This is that [which] the most part of writers do declare, touching Alexander's demand, and the oracles given him. Yet did Alexander himself write unto his mother that he had secret oracles from the god, which he would only impart unto her at his return into Macedon.

[Others say that the priest, desirous as a piece of courtesy to address him in Greek by saying "O Paidion" [dear son], by a slip in pronunciation ended with the "s" instead of the "n," and said "O Paidios" [son of Jupiter], which mistake Alexander was well enough pleased with, and it went for current that the oracle had called him so.] Whereupon there ran a rumour straight among his men, that Jupiter had called him his son.

Part Three

It is said also, that he heard Psammon the philosopher in Egypt, and that he liked his words very well, when he said that God was king of of all mortal men: "For," (quoth he), "he that commandeth all things must needs be God." But Alexander himself spake better, and like a philosopher, when he said that God generally was father to all mortal men, but that particularly he did elect the best sort for himself. To conclude, he showed himself more arrogant unto the barbarous people, and made as though he certainly believed that he had been begotten of some god: but unto the Grecians he spake more modestly of **divine generation**.

For in a letter he wrote unto the Athenians touching the city of Samos, he said: "I gave ye not that noble free city, but it was given you, at that time, by him whom they called my lord and father": meaning Philip. Afterwards also, being stricken with an arrow and feeling great pain of it: "My friends," said he, "This blood which is spilt is man's blood, and not as Homer said: 'No such as from the immortal gods doth flow.'"

[*short omission*]

Narration and Discussion

How did Alexander "profit himself much by Homer in this journey?"

How did the soothsayers reassure Alexander after the birds ate up his plans for the city?

For older students: Plutarch says, "But Alexander himself spake better, and like a philosopher, when he said that God generally was father to all mortal men, but that particularly he did elect the best sort for himself." Compare this with Christian beliefs (e.g. John 3:16).

Was Alexander's strength and success truly due to his courage? Was it the favouring of "Fortune," or was there something else behind it?

Lesson Ten

Introduction

This lesson moves from the imagined tragedies at a drama contest to the real grief of Darius at the loss of his queen. Surprisingly, this gave Darius less desire for increased anger at Alexander (who had caused their separation), but rather more respect for him. However, since Alexander had rejected Darius' negotiations for a peaceful sharing of the Persian empire, the only possible response was a final battle.

Vocabulary

tragedies: theatrical performances

pastimes: events and performances, often in honour of the gods (and carrying more significance than our "pastimes")

strived: motivated

kings of the Cyprians: Alexander had conquered Cyprus, and its rulers were now his subjects

setters forth of them: financial sponsors

furnish: sponsor, back

players: actors

ten talents: a sum of money

without dissimulation: without any pretense

eunuch: a certain type of male servant

Alexander

On the Map

Alexander ended his Egyptian journey, retraced his route back to Tyre, headed east through Damascus, and eventually crossed the Euphrates.

Reading

Part One

Returning out of Egypt into Phoenicia, he made many sacrifices, feasts, and processions in honour of the gods: sundry dances, **tragedies**, and such like **pastimes** goodly to behold, not only for the sumptuous setting out of them, but also for the goodwill and diligence of the **setters forth of them**, which **strived** everyone to exceed the other. For the **kings of the Cyprians** were the setters of them forth, as at Athens they draw by lot a citizen of every tribe of the people, to defray the charges of these pastimes. These kings were very earnest who should do best, but specially Nicocreon, king of Salamis, and Pasicrates, lord of the city of Soli. For it fell to their lot to **furnish** two of the excellentest **players**: Pasicrates furnished Athenodorus, and Nicocreon, Thessalus. [Thessalus was most favoured by Alexander, though it did not appear till Athenodorus was declared victor by the plurality of votes.] For when he went from the plays, he told them he did like the judges' opinion well; notwithstanding, he would have been contented to have given the one half of his realm not to have seen Thessalus overcome. [However, when he understood Athenodorus was fined by the Athenians for being absent at the festivals of Bacchus, though he refused his request that he would write a letter in his behalf, he gave him a sufficient sum to satisfy the penalty.] Also, when Lycon [of] Scarphia, an excellent stage player, had pleased Alexander well and did [slip] in a verse in his comedy [in which he begged for a present] of **ten talents**: Alexander, laughing at it, gave it [to] him.

Part Two

Darius at that time wrote unto Alexander, and unto certain of his friends also, to pray him to take ten thousand talents for the ransom of all those prisoners he had in his hands, [*offering him also*] all the countries on this side [of] the river Euphrates, and one of his daughters also in marriage, that from thenceforth he might be his kinsman and friend. Alexander imparted this to his council.

Amongst them, Parmenio said unto him: "If I were Alexander," quoth he, "surely I would accept this offer." "So would I indeed," quoth Alexander again, "if I were Parmenio."

In fine, he wrote again unto Darius that if he would submit himself, he would use him courteously: if not, that then he would presently march towards him. But he repented him afterwards, when King Darius' wife [*named Statira*] was dead with child. For **without dissimulation** it grieved him much, that he had lost so noble an occasion to shew his courtesy and clemency. This notwithstanding, he gave her body honourable burial, sparing for no cost.

[Among the **eunuchs** who waited in the queen's chamber and were taken prisoners with the women, there was one Tireus, who, getting out of the camp, fled away on horseback to Darius, to inform him of his wife's death.] Then Darius beating of his head, and weeping bitterly, cried out aloud: "Oh gods! what wretched hap have the Persians! that have not only had the wife and sister of their king taken prisoners even in his lifetime, but now that she is dead also in travail of child, she hath been deprived of princely burial!"

Then spake the eunuch to him, and said:

> "For her burial, most gracious King, and for all due honour that might be wished her, Persia hath no cause to complain of her hard fortune. For neither did Queen Statira your wife, whilst she lived prisoner, nor your mother nor daughters, want any part or jot of their honour they were wont to have before, saving only to see the light of your honour, the which the god Oromasdes [will] grant to restore again (if it be his will) unto your Majesty: neither was there any honour wanting at her death (to set forth her stately funerals) that might be gotten, but more was lamented also with the tears of your enemies. For Alexander is as merciful in victory as he is valiant in battle."

Darius, being vexed in mind for very grief, took the eunuch aside into the secretest place of his tent, and [*asked him to swear that his wife had not been dishonoured by Alexander.*]

[*omission*]

Then Darius coming out among his friends again, holding up his hands unto the heavens, made this prayer unto the gods:

> "O heavenly gods, creators of men, and protectors of kings and realms: First, I beseech you, grant me that restoring the Persians again to their former good state, I may leave the realm unto my successors, with that glory and fame I received it of my predecessors; that obtaining victory, I may use Alexander with that great honour and courtesy which he hath in my misery shown unto those I loved best in the world. Or otherwise, if the time appointed be come that the kingdom of Persia must needs have end, either through divine revenge, or by natural change of earthly things: then good gods yet grant that none but Alexander after me may sit in Cyrus' throne."

Divers writers do agree that these things came even thus to pass.

Narration and Discussion

Why did the Macedonians stage dramatic contests and other "pastimes" at that time?

Why did Alexander reject the offers from King Darius?

Why was Tireus so anxious to tell Darius that his wife had received proper treatment and a royal funeral? Might he not instead have wished to cast a negative light on Alexander?

The Plutarch Project

Lesson Eleven

Introduction

Plutarch leads up to the Battle of Gaugamela by describing some playfighting which got out of hand, but which also foreshadowed Alexander's victory.

Vocabulary

heated with contention: hot-headed and ready to fight

The servants who followed the camp: this is Dryden's phrase. North translates it "the slaves of his army."

he confided in: he had confidence in

worsted: beaten

munition: weapons

out of their battle: out of formation

carriage: weapons and other supplies

girt close about him: close-fitting

People

Philotas, Parmenio: see introductory notes

Historic Occasions

October, 331 B.C.: Battle of **Gaugamela**

On the Map

Alexander continued eastward, crossing the Euphrates, heading somewhat north to cross the Tigris, following the Tigris for a distance,

Reading

Part One

Now Alexander having conquered all Asia this side of the Euphrates, he went to meet with Darius, [who] came down with ten hundred thousand fighting men [Dryden: *a million of men*]. [In his march a very ridiculous passage happened. **The servants who followed the camp**, for sport's sake, divided themselves into two parties, and named the commander of one of them Alexander, and the other Darius. At first they only pelted one another with clods of earth, but presently took to their fists, and at last, **heated with contention**, they fought in good earnest with stones and clubs, so that they had much ado to part them; till Alexander, upon hearing of it, ordered the two captains to decide the quarrel by single combat, and armed him who bore his name himself, while **Philotas** did the same to him who represented Darius.] All the army thereupon was gathered together to see this combat between them, as a thing that did betoken good or ill luck to some. The fight was sharp between them, but in the end, he that was called Alexander overcame the other. Alexander, to reward him, gave him twelve villages, [with leave to wear the Persian dress]. Thus it is written by Eratosthenes.

Part Two

The great battle that Alexander fought with Darius, was not (as many writers report) at Arbela, but at **Gaugamela**, which signifieth in the Persian tongue, the house of the camel. For some one of the ancient kings of Persia that had escaped from the hands of his enemies, fleeing upon a [swift] camel, lodged him in that place, and therefore appointed the revenues of certain villages to keep the camel there.

There fell out at that time an eclipse of the moon, in the month called Boedromion (now August), about the time that the Feast of the Mysteries was celebrated at Athens. The eleventh night after that, both their armies being in sight of the other, Darius kept his men in battle array, and went himself by torchlight, viewing his bands and companies. Alexander, on the other side, whilst his Macedonian soldiers slept, was before his tent with Aristander the soothsayer; and made certain secret ceremonies and sacrifices unto Apollo [Dryden: *the god Fear*].

The [oldest] captains of the Macedonians, specially **Parmenio**, seeing all the valley betwixt the river of Niphates, and the mountains of the Gordyaeans, all on a bright light with the fires of the barbarous people, and hearing a dreadful noise as of a confused multitude of people that filled their camp with the sound thereof: they were amazed, and [concluded] that in one day it was in manner impossible to fight a battle with such an incredible multitude of people.

Thereupon they went unto Alexander after he had ended his ceremonies, and did counsel him to give battle by night, because the darkness thereof should help to keep all fear from his men, which the sight of their enemies would bring them into. [To this he gave them the celebrated answer, "I will not steal a victory." Some at the time thought [it] a boyish and inconsiderate speech, as if he played with danger. Others, however, regarded [it] as evidence that **he confided in** his present condition, and acted on a true judgment of the future, not wishing to leave Darius, in case he were **worsted**, the pretext of trying his fortune again, which he might suppose himself to have, if he could impute his overthrow to the disadvantage of the night, as he did before to the mountains, the narrow passages, and the sea.] "For," said he, "Darius will never leave to make wars with us for lack of men, nor **munition**, having so large a realm as he hath, and such a world of people besides: but then he will no more hazard battle, when his heart is done, and all hope taken from him, and that he seeth his army at noonday overthrown by plain battle."

After his captains were gone from him, he went into his tent, and laid him down to sleep, and slept all that night more soundly than he was wont to do before: insomuch as the lords and princes of his camp coming to wait upon him at his uprising, marvelled when they found him so sound asleep, and therefore of themselves they commanded the soldiers to eat. Afterwards, perceiving that time came fast upon them, Parmenio went into Alexander's chamber, and coming to his bedside, called him twice or thrice by his name, till at the last he waked him and asked him how it chanced that he slept so long, like one that had already overcome, and that did not think he should fight as great and dangerous a battle as ever he did in his life. ["And are we not so, indeed," replied Alexander, smiling, "since we are at last relieved from the trouble of wandering in pursuit of Darius through a wide and wasted country, hoping in vain that he would fight us?"]

Part Three

Now Alexander did not only shew himself before the battle, but even at the very instant of battle, a noble man of courage and of great judgment. For Parmenio leading the left wing of his battle, the men of arms of the Bactrians gave such a fierce onset upon the Macedonians that they made them give back: and Mazeus also, King Darius' lieutenant, sent certain troops of horsemen **out of their battle** to give charge upon them that were left in the camp to guard the **carriage**.

[This so disturbed Parmenio that he sent messengers to acquaint Alexander that the camp and baggage would be all lost, unless he immediately relieved the rear by a considerable reinforcement drawn out of the front.] When this news came to Alexander from Parmenio, he had already given the signal of battle unto his men to give charge. Whereupon he answered the messenger that brought him these news, that he should tell Parmenio he was a madman and out of his wits, not remembering that if they won the battle, they should not only save their own carriage, but also win the carriage of their enemies: and if it were their chance to lose it, then that they should not need to care for their carriage, nor for their slaves, but only to think to die honourably, valiantly fighting for his life.

Having sent this message unto Parmenio, he put on his helmet. [The rest of his armour for his body, he had put it on before in his tent, which were a coat of the Sicilian make, **girt close about him**, and over that a breast-piece of thickly quilted linen, which was taken among other booty at the Battle of Issus.] His headpiece was as bright as silver, made by Theophilus the armourer: his collar [of the same metal], all set full of precious stones, and he had a sword by his side, marvellous light, and of excellent temper, which the king of the Citieians had given him, using commonly to fight with his sword at any set battle. His coat armour was marvellous rich, and of sumptuous workmanship, far above all the rest he wore. It was of the workmanship of Hellicon, which the Rhodians gave him for a present, and this he commonly wore when he went to battle.

Now when he did set his men in battle array, or made any oration unto them, or did ride alongst the bands to take view of them: he always used to ride upon another horse to spare Bucephalus, because he was then somewhat old: notwithstanding, when he meant indeed to fight, then Bucephalus was brought unto him, and as soon as he was gotten up on his back, the trumpet sounded, and he gave charge.

Then, after he had made long exhortations to encourage the men of arms of the Thessalians, and the other Grecians also, and when they had all promised him they would stick to him like men, and prayed him to lead them, and give charge upon the enemies: he took his lance in his left hand, and holding up his right hand unto heaven, besought the gods (as Callisthenes writeth) that if it were true he was begotten of Jupiter, that it would please them that day to help him, and to encourage the Grecians. The soothsayer Aristander was then a-horseback hard by Alexander, appareled all in white, and a crown of gold on his head, who showed Alexander, when he made his prayer, an eagle flying over his head and pointing directly towards his enemies. This marvellously encouraged all the army that saw it, and with this joy, the men of arms of Alexander's side, encouraging one another, did set spurs to their horse to charge upon the enemies.

Narration and Discussion

How did the sham battles between "Alexander" and "Darius" get out of hand? How were they resolved?

"I will not steal a victory." What did Alexander mean?

Why was Alexander able to sleep so well the night before the battle?

How did Alexander show himself to be "a noble man of courage, and of great judgment?"

For those interested in military strategy: There are various opinions about whether Alexander meant to trick Darius by taking an unexpected northern route to Gaugamela, or whether he chose it to avoid heat and have better access to food. There are also questions

Alexander

about why that part of the Tigris was undefended, and the Macedonians were able to cross it without trouble. Was Darius merely careless, or was he leading Alexander into a trap by choosing a battlefield that (he thought) suited his strengths?

Lesson Twelve

Introduction

This lesson ends the story of the Battle of Gaugamela, which marked Alexander's victory over the Persian Empire. It also introduces his new status as "King of Asia."

Vocabulary

battle: battle formation

dispersed themselves: broke ranks and ran away

let, hinder: get in the way or prevent

continue the execution: continue what they were doing

every man thought: that is, thought correctly; understood.

naphtha, bitumen: Bitumen is asphalt, and it was used in the ancient world for many purposes including mummification. The naphtha shown to Alexander may have been a crude oil version of the thicker, stickier bitumen. North spells it "naptha," but as that now commonly refers to mineral spirits, I have used "naphtha."

unctuous: oily

peradventure: perhaps

tincture: dye mixture

People

Phayllos the wrestler: Phayllos of Croton, an athlete who also commanded a ship at the Battle of Salamis in 480 B.C.

Harpalus: see introductory notes

On the Map

After the battle of Gaugamela, Alexander headed south to Babylon, and east to Susa. He marched a long way to the northwest to arrive at **Ecbatana**; then, it appears, he returned south.

Reading

Part One

The **battle** of the footmen of the Persians began a little to give way, and before the foremost could come to give them charge, the barbarous people turned their backs, and fled. The chase was great, Alexander driving them that fled upon the midst of their own **battle**, where Darius himself was in person. He spied him afar off over the foremost ranks, in the midst of his [life-guard], being a goodly tall prince, standing in a chariot of war, compassed in round with great troops of horsemen, all set in goodly ordinance to receive the enemy. But when they saw Alexander at hand with so grim a look, chasing them that fled through those that yet kept their ranks: there fell such a fear among them, that the most part **dispersed themselves**. Notwithstanding, the best and most valiantest men fought it out to the death before their king, and falling dead one upon another, they did **let** them that the enemies could not so well follow Darius. For they, lying one by another on the ground, drawing on to the last gasp, did yet take both men and horses by the legs to **hinder** them.

Darius then seeing nothing but terror and destruction before his eyes, and that the bands which he had set before him for safeguard came back upon him so as he could not devise how to turn his chariot forward nor backward, the wheels were so hindered and stayed with the heaps of dead bodies, and that the horse[s] also being set upon and [almost hidden] in this conflict, fell to leaping and plunging for fear, so that the charioteers could no longer guide nor drive them: he got up upon a mare that lately had foaled, and so saved himself, fleeing upon her. And yet [he would not have] thus escaped, had not Parmenio once again sent unto Alexander to pray him to come and aid him: because there was yet a great squadron [of Persians] that made no countenance to flee. Somewhat there was in it, that they accused Parmenio that day to have dealt but slackly and cowardly, either because his age had taken his courage from him, or else for that he envied Alexander's greatness and prosperity, who against his [Parmenio's] will became over-great, as Callisthenes said. [Alexander, though he was not a little vexed to be so recalled and hindered from pursuing his victory, yet concealed the true reason from his men, and causing a retreat to be sounded, as if it were too late to **continue the execution** any longer, marched back towards the place of danger.] Notwithstanding, news came to him by the way that in that place also they had given the enemies the overthrow, and that they fled every way for life.

The battle having this success, **every man thought** that the kingdom of the Persians was utterly overthrown, and that Alexander likewise was become king of all Asia: whereupon he made sumptuous sacrifices unto the gods, and gave great riches, houses, lands and possessions unto his friends and familiars. Furthermore, to show his liberality also unto the Grecians, he wrote unto them that he would have all tyrannies suppressed throughout all Greece, and that all the Grecians should live at liberty under their own laws. Particularly also he wrote unto the Plataeians, that he would re-edify their city again, because their predecessors in time past, had given their country unto the Grecians, to fight against the barbarous people for the defence of the common liberty of all Greece.

He sent also into, Italy unto the Crotonians, part of the spoil, to [honour **Phayllos the wrestler**] who in the time of the wars with the Medes (when all the Grecians that dwelt in Italy had forsaken their natural countrymen of Greece itself, because they thought they could not otherwise escape), went with a ship of his unto Salamis, which he armed and set forth at his own charges, because he would be at the battle and partake also of the common danger with the Grecians. Such honour did Alexander bear unto prowess, that he loved to reward and remember the worthy deeds of men.

Then Alexander marching with his army into the country of Babylon, they all yielded straight unto him.

Part Two (optional)

[In **Ecbatana** he was much surprised at the sight of the place where fire issues in a continuous stream, like a spring of water, out of a cleft in the earth, and the stream of **naphtha**, which, not far from this spot, flows out so abundantly as to form a sort of lake. This naphtha, in other respects resembling **bitumen**, is so subject to take fire, that before it touches the flame it will kindle at the very light that surrounds it, and often inflame the intermediate air also.] The barbarous people of that country, being desirous to show Alexander the nature of that naphtha, scattered the street that led to his lodging with some of it. Then the day being shut in, they fired it at one of the ends, and the first drops taking fire, in the twinkling of an eye, all the rest from one end of the street to the other was of a flame, and though it was dark and within night, lightened all the place thereabout.

[*Omission: a sadistic experiment with naphtha*]

The manner, however, of the production of naphtha admits of a diversity of opinion…of whether this liquid substance that feeds the flame does not rather proceed from a soil that is **unctuous** and productive of fire, as that of the province of Babylon is, where the ground is so very hot that oftentimes the grains of barley leap up and are thrown out, as if the violent inflammation had made the earth throb: and in the extreme heats the inhabitants are wont to sleep upon skins filled with water.] **Harpalus**, whom Alexander left there [as] his lieutenant and governor of that country, desiring to set forth and beautify the gardens of the king's palace and walks of the same with all manner of plants of Greece: he brought all the rest to good pass, saving ivy only, which the earth could never abide, but it ever died, because the heat and temper of the earth killed it, and the ivy of itself liketh fresh air and a cold ground. This digression is somewhat from the matter, but **peradventure** the reader will not think it troublesome, how hard soever he [might] find it, so it be not over-tedious.

Part Three

Alexander having won the city of Susa, he found within the castle four thousand talents [Dryden: *forty thousand*] in ready coin, gold and silver, besides other infinite treasure [of inestimable value], amongst the which (it is said) he found to the value of five thousand talents' weight of [Hermonian purple, that had been laid up there [for a] hundred and ninety years and yet kept its colour as fresh and lively as at first. The reason of which, they say, is that in dyeing the purple they made use of honey and of white oil in the white **tincture**, both which after the like space of time preserve the clearness and brightness of their lustre.

Dinon also relates that the Persian kings had water fetched from the Nile and the Danube, which they did lock up with their other treasure[s] for a confirmation of the greatness of their empire, and to show that they were lords of the world.

Narration and Discussion

How did Alexander commemorate his victory at Gaugamela?

The Persian kings seemed to have collected every kind of rich manmade treasure. But at the end of the lesson, Plutarch quotes a historian who said that Persian kings also collected natural treasures to show their ownership over the earth. If you have a nature collection, what does it mean to you? What other things might one collect that cost nothing?

Scientific narration: The naphtha demonstrations fall into the "don't try this at home" category, but older students may be interested in the technical aspects of this lesson, such as the topic of flammability.

Examination Questions for Term One

Younger Students:

1. Write an account of Alexander the Great and Bucephalus.
2. How did Alexander behave when ill towards his physician?

The Plutarch Project

Older Students:

1. Describe (a) the meeting of Alexander with Diogenes, and (b) how Alexander crossed the Granicus River.

2. How did Alexander spend his days at a time of leisure?

3. (Alternative) Describe (a) the personal appearance, and (b) the early education of Alexander.

Alexander

Lesson Thirteen

Introduction

If you are returning to the *Life of Alexander* after a break, take a few minutes to review the previous term's work, especially the victory at Gaugamela, where King Darius of Persia was defeated but escaped from the Macedonians. Remember, however, that it is more important to gain an understanding of Alexander's character than it is to recall every historical detail.

As we begin the second half of this *Life*, "the kingdom of the Persians was utterly overthrown," but the Macedonian army had not yet entered central Persia or captured Darius. **Lesson Thirteen** opens with a battle at the Persian Gates (a mountain pass leading into the central part of the country).

Vocabulary

wardrobe: treasure

sometime: in past times

familiars: friends

with such sport: so casually

repent him: feel sorry for what he had done

give good countenance…: Dryden translates this as "accompanying what he gave with that courtesy and freedom which, to speak truth, is necessary to make a benefit really obliging."

People

Xerxes: a great Persian king

Demaratus [the] Corinthian: It seems likely that this is the same Demaratus who had fought with Timoleon in Sicily (see the *Life of Timoleon*, **Lessons Seven** and **Nine**).

Ariobarzanes: His name does not appear in Plutarch's text, but he was satrap (governor) of the southern part of the Persian empire, and he commanded troops at the Battle of Gaugamela. He also headed the Persian defense at the Persian Gates, but he was killed either there or directly afterwards at Persepolis.

Thaïs: a romantic companion of Ptolemy, and possibly also of Alexander

Ptolemy I Soter: see introductory notes

Historic Occasions

330 B.C.: Battle of the Persian Gates

Reading

Part One

[The entrance into Persia was through a most difficult country, and was guarded by the noblest of the Persians, Darius himself having escaped further.] There was one that spake the Greek and Persian tongue (whose father was born in the country of Lycia, and his mother a Persian) that guided Alexander into Persia, [by a way something about, yet without fetching any considerable compass].

[*brief omission*]

There was then great slaughter made in Persia of the prisoners that were taken. For Alexander himself writeth that he commanded the men should be put to the sword, thinking that the best way to serve his turn. It is said also that in Persepolis he found a marvellous treasure of gold and silver in ready money, as he had done before in the city of Susa: which he carried away with all the rest of the king's rich **wardrobe**, and [loaded it on] ten thousand mules and five thousand camels.

[Amongst other things, he happened to observe a large statue of **Xerxes** thrown carelessly down to the ground in the confusion made by the multitude of soldiers pressing into the palace.] Thereupon he

Alexander

stayed, and spake unto it as if it had been alive, saying: "I cannot tell whether I should pass by thee, and let thee lie, for the war thou madest **sometime** against the Grecians; or whether I should lift thee up, respecting the noble mind and virtues thou hadst." In the end, when he had stood mute a long time, considering of it, he went his way: and, meaning to refresh his weary army, because it was the winter quarter, he remained there four months together.

The report goeth that the first time that Alexander sat under the [canopy] of King Darius, all of rich gold: **Demaratus [the] Corinthian**, [who was much attached to him and had been one of his father's friends], burst out in tears for joy, good old man, saying that the Grecians long time dead before were deprived of this blessed hap, to see Alexander set in King Xerxes' princely chair.

Part Two

After that, preparing again to go against Darius, he would needs make merry one day, and refresh himself with some banquet. It chanced so, that he with his companions was bidden to a private feast, where [there were assembled his followers and some women]. Amongst them was that famous **Thaïs**, born in the country of Attica, and then [mistress of **Ptolemy**, who was afterwards king of Egypt.]

[*As the feasting and drinking went on, Thaïs made the suggestion, half-serious, half-joking, that they should burn down Xerxes' palace to avenge his burning of the Temple of Athena in 480 B.C.*]

When she had said [this], Alexander's **familiars** about him clapped their hands, and made great noise for joy, saying that it [would be] as good a deed as could be possible, and persuaded Alexander unto it. Alexander, yielding to their persuasions, rose up, and putting a garland of flowers upon his head, went foremost himself; and all his familiars followed after him, crying and dancing all about the castle. The other Macedonians, hearing of it also, came thither immediately with torchlight and great joy, hoping that this was a good sign that Alexander meant to return again into Macedon, and not to dwell in the country of the barbarous people, since he did burn and destroy the king's castle. Thus, and in this sort, it was thought to be burnt. Some writers think otherwise: that it was not burnt **with such sport**, but by determination of the council. But howsoever it was, all they grant that Alexander did presently **repent him**, and commanded the fire to be quenched straight.

Part Three

[Alexander's] liberality, that good will and readiness to give, increased with his conquests: and when he did bestow gifts [to] any, he would besides his gift ever **give good countenance [to those] on whom he bestowed his grace and favour**.

[*one example omitted for length*]

Another time, he met with a poor Macedonian that led a mule laden with gold of the kings: and when the poor mule was so weary that she could no longer carry her burden, the muleteer put it [*the burden*] upon his own back, and loaded himself withal, carrying it so a good pretty way; howbeit in the end being overladen, [he] was about to throw it down on the ground. Alexander perceiving it, asked him what burden he carried. When it was told him: "Well," quoth he to the muleteer, "be not weary yet, but carry it into [your own] tent, for I give it thee." To be short, he was angrier with them that would take nothing of him, than he was with those that would ask him [for something].

[*omission: mature content*]

The goods and riches he gave unto his familiars and guard about him were very great, as it appeareth plainly by a letter which his mother Olympias wrote unto him, to this effect: "I know thou sparest not to give thy friends large gifts, and that thou makest much of them: but thereby thou makest them king's fellows; they get many friends, and [in the meantime you leave yourself destitute]."

[*further omissions*]

[To his mother he sent many presents but would never suffer her to meddle with matters of state or war, not indulge her busy temper, and when she fell out with him on this account, he bore her ill humour very patiently. Nay, more, when he read a long letter from Antipater full of accusations against her, "Antipater," he said, "does not know that one tear of a mother effaces a thousand such letters as these."]

Narration and Discussion

How was Alexander's army finally able to get through the Persian Gates?

Was Alexander truly generous, or did he have other reasons for giving lavishly to others?

What sort of relationship did Alexander have with his mother?

For older students: Is an action such as the slaughter of the prisoners ever justified? What does this decision show about Alexander?

Lesson Fourteen

Introduction

This lesson continues the previous discussion of Alexander's generosity, showing examples now of the concern he showed for his friends when they were in trouble, and his scorn for those who chose pampering and luxury over courage and action. But his new status as King of Asia made things more complicated.

Vocabulary

dissolute and licentious: wild, unbridled

chamberlains: personal servants

travail: labour, work hard

vile: in this context it means worthless or of little value

for slothful curiosity's sake: from squeamishness

the type: the ideal, the model

hardness: toughness, discipline

ichneumon: possibly a mythical beast known as the "enemy of the dragon"; it can also mean a mongoose or otter

hellebore: a genus of plants, often used as medicine in the ancient world, but known to be somewhat toxic

flight: escape

stayed and taken: captured

bondman: slave

People

Philotas: a son of Parmenio; see introductory notes

Hephaestion, Seleucus, Craterus: see introductory notes

Historic Occasions

324-323 B.C.: Harpalus' escape

Reading

Part One

Furthermore, Alexander perceiving, on a time, that his friends became very **dissolute and licentious** in diet and life; and that Agnon Teian had his corked shoes nailed with silver nails; that Leonatus also caused divers camels to be laden amongst his carriage with powder of Egypt, to put upon him when he wrestled or used any other exercise of body; and that also they carried after **Philotas** [nets] for chase and hunting, of a hundred furlongs long; and that there were [men in his camp] also that used precious perfumes and sweet savours when they bathed themselves, more than there were that rubbed themselves with plain oil; and that they had fine **chamberlains** to rub them in the bath, and to make their beds soft and delicate: he wisely and courteously rebuked them and said [*the following*].

> "I marvel," said he, "that you, which have fought in so often and great battles, do not remember that they which **travail** do sleep more sweet[ly] and soundly than they that take their ease and do nothing; and that you do not mark that, comparing your life with the manner of the life of the Persians, to live at pleasure is a **vile** thing, and to travail is princely. And how I pray you, can a man take pain to dress his own horse, or to make clean his lance or helmet, that **for slothful curiosity's sake** disdaineth to rub his own body with his fine fingers? Are you ignorant that **the type** of honour in all our victory consisteth in scorning to do that which we see them do whom we have vanquished and overcome?"

To bring them therefore by his example to acquaint themselves with **hardness**, he took more pains in wars and in hunting, and did hazard himself more dangerously, than ever he had done before.

[*short omission*]

This notwithstanding, his friends and familiars having wealth at will, as men exceeding rich, they would needs live delicately and at ease, and would take no more pains, misliking utterly to go up and down the countries to make war here and there: and thereupon began a little to find fault with Alexander, and to speak evil of him. Which at the first Alexander took quietly, saying, that it was honour for a king to suffer himself to be slandered and ill-spoken of, for doing of good.

Part Two

And yet the least good turns he did unto his friends did show his hearty love and honour he bare them, as shall appear unto you by some examples that follow. Peucestas, being bitten by a bear, did let his friends understand it by letters, but he wrote nothing thereof unto Alexander. Alexander was offended therewith and wrote unto him thus: "Send me word at the least [of] how thou doest, and whether any of thy fellows did forsake thee at the hunting, to the end they may be punished."

Hephaestion being absent about certain business he had, Alexander wrote unto him that as they were hunting a beast called an *ichneumon*, **Craterus** unfortunately crossing Perdiccas' dart was stricken through both his thighs. Peucestas being cured of a great disease, Alexander wrote unto Alexippus his physician that had cured him and gave him thanks. Craterus also being sick, he dreamed of him one night, and therefore made certain sacrifices for the recovery of his health, and sent unto him, willing him to do the like. And when the physician Pausanias meant to give him [Craterus] a drink of **hellebore**, he wrote letters unto him, telling him what danger he was in, and prayed him to be careful how he received that medicine.

[He was so tender of his friends' reputations that he imprisoned those who brought him the first news of Harpalus' **flight** and withdrawal from his service, as if they had falsely accused him.]

[*omission*]

It is a wonderful thing to see what pains he would take, to write for his friends, even in such trifles as he did. As when he wrote into Cilicia for a servant of **Seleucus** that was fled from his master, sending straight commandment that they should carefully lay for him. And by another letter he commendeth Peucestas, for that he had **stayed and taken** one Nicon, a slave of **Craterus**. And by one other letter also unto Megabizus, touching another **bondman** that had taken sanctuary in a temple: he commanded him also to seek to entice him out of the sanctuary, to lay hold on him if he could, but otherwise not to meddle with him in any case.

It is said also, that at the first when he used to sit in judgment to hear criminal causes, whilst the accuser went on with his complaint and accusation: he always used to lay his hand upon one of his ears to keep that clean from the matter of accusation, thereby reserving it to hear the purgation and justification of the person condemned. But afterwards, the number of accusations that were brought before him did so provoke and alter him that he did believe the false accusations, by the great number of the true that were brought in. But nothing put him more in rage than when he understood they had spoken ill of him: and then he was so fierce as no pardon would be granted, for that he loved his honour more than his kingdom or life.

Narration and Discussion

"To live at pleasure is a **vile** thing, and to **travail** is princely." Some people think quite the opposite. What did Alexander mean?

How did Alexander show that he cared for his friends?

For older students: Charlotte Mason said that those who act with Will are those who have a purpose outside of themselves, but that those who act with Willfulness are bound by their appetites (we might say they need immediate gratification). How did Alexander's impatience with those who lived "delicately and at ease" illustrate this principle?

Lesson Fifteen

Introduction

This lesson is all about water! The Macedonians nearly perished from thirst on a long march; the last moments of King Darius' life were eased by a drink of water offered by an enemy; and Alexander reached the Caspian Sea.

Vocabulary

he went against Darius: the goal was to overtake the enemy camp

flying away at all adventure: running for their lives

they ran upon the spur: they rushed

almost at the last cast: almost dead

mishap: misfortune, bad luck

I cannot requite thee: I cannot pay you back

gave up the ghost: died

all the flower of his army: his best soldiers

he did use them: he treated them

People

Bessus: a Persian satrap (a high official) and military commander who conspired to capture and overthrow Darius after the Battle of Gaugamela. It appears that the conspirators intended to hand him over to Alexander; but when the Macedonians appeared at the Persian camp, they panicked, stabbed Darius, and then fled. Bessus, who was a cousin of Darius and was next in line to the throne, called himself King Artaxerxes V after the death of Darius; but he was soon captured and executed by Alexander.

Polystratus: a Macedonian soldier

Historic Occasions

330 B.C.: the death of Darius

329 B.C.: the death of Bessus

On the Map

In Part One, Alexander followed Darius into the desert area of Rhagae (east of modern-day Tehran). In Part Two, the Macedonians travelled to the region of **Hyrcania**, near the Caspian Sea (**the sea Caspium**).

Reading

Part One

Then at that time **he went against Darius**, thinking that he meant to fight again: but, understanding that **Bessus** had taken him, he then gave the Thessalians leave to depart home into their country, and gave them two thousand talents over and above their ordinary pay. [In this long and painful pursuit of Darius, for eleven days he marched thirty-three hundred furlongs, (and it) harassed his soldiers so that most of them were ready to give it up, chiefly for want of water.]

It chanced him one day to meet with certain Macedonians that carried (upon mules) goatskins full of water, which they had fetched from a river. They, seeing Alexander in manner dead for thirst, [it] being about noon, ran quickly to him and in a [helmet] brought him water. Alexander asked them to whom they carried this water. They answered him again that they carried it to their children, and said, "but yet we would have Your Grace to live: for though we lose them, we may get more children."

When they had said so, Alexander took the helmet with water, and perceiving that men of arms that were about him and had followed him did thrust out their necks to look upon this water, he gave the water back again unto them that had given it him, and thanked them, but drank none of it. "For," said he, "if I drink alone, all these men here will faint." Then they, seeing the noble courage and courtesy of Alexander, cried out that he should lead them: and therewithal began to spur their horses, saying that they were not weary nor athirst, nor did think themselves mortal, so long as they had such a king.

Every man was alike willing to follow Alexander; yet had he but three score only that entered with him into the enemies' camp. There, passing over much gold and silver which was scattered abroad in the marketplace, and going also by many chariots full of women and children, which they found in the fields, **flying away at all adventure: they ran upon the spur** until they had overtaken the foremost that fled, thinking to have found Darius amongst them. But at the length, with much ado, they found him laid along in a coach, having many wounds upon his body, some of darts and some [of] spears. So he, being **almost at the last cast**, called for some drink, and drank cold water which **Polystratus** gave him. To whom when he had drunk, he said: "This is my last **mishap**, my friend, that having received this pleasure, **I cannot requite thee**: howbeit Alexander will recompense thee, and the gods [will recompense] Alexander for the liberality and courtesy which he hath shewed unto my wife and children, whom I pray thee embrace for my sake." At these last words, he took Polystratus by the hand, and so **gave up the ghost**. Alexander came immediately after, and plainly shewed that he was sorry for his death and misfortune; and undoing his own cloak, he cast it upon the body of Darius.

[omission: the cruel execution of Bessus]

Then Alexander having given Darius' corpse princely burial and [having] embalmed him: he sent it unto his mother and received his brother Exathres for one of his friends.

Part Two

From thence he went into the country of **Hyrcania** with **all the flower of his army**, where he saw the gulf of **the sea Caspium**, which he thought of no less greatness than the **sea of Pontus [Dryden: Euxine]**, howbeit calmer than the other seas be.

[short omission about the sea]

As Alexander went through the country, certain barbarous people suddenly set upon them that led Bucephalus his horse, and took him: but with that he was in such a rage, that he sent a herald into their country to proclaim open wars upon them, and [said] that he would put man, woman, and child to the sword, if they brought him not his horse again. Whereupon, when his horse was returned home, and that they yielded up their cities and forts into his hands: **he did use them** all very courteously, and moreover did give them money for the ransom of his horse, which they restored.

Narration and Discussion

"For," said he, "if I drink alone, all these men here will faint." How did Alexander show true leadership in this situation?

Who showed the most compassion for others in this lesson?

For older students: In one sense, the conspirators had done Alexander a favour by capturing and killing Darius; and with Alexander's growing power, even Bessus might not have posed much of a threat as king of what was left of Persia; or he might have easily been conquered in battle. Discuss why it was (or was not) necessary to punish the conspirators so severely. (**Creative narration:** This could be debated in a group, or written as an editorial.)

Lesson Sixteen

Introduction

Scholars have debated the details of what Alexander wore as King of Asia. What did each piece of clothing symbolize to the Persians, to the Macedonians, and to Alexander himself? The key seems to be that he did not want to be viewed as merely following Darius, so he deliberately left off the **tiara** or headdress associated with Persian kings. Median-style loose trousers made the Macedonians think of theatrical costumes, and were also sometimes worn by women, so Alexander avoided those. He did, however, incorporate a regal tunic; a Persian-style belt, which symbolized power; and a diadem crown into his wardrobe.

Vocabulary

apparel himself...: dress in the Persian style

Medes: the people of Media, a kingdom which had been conquered by the Persians. Plutarch refers here to the Median style of riding dress.

strange: foreign to them

sleeved vest: loose jacket

tiara: in this context, a type of headdress associated with Persian royalty

Persian mode and the Macedonian: Plutarch's Greek text has "Median" instead of "Macedonian," and North also says "Medes," but later translators agreed that "Macedonian" made more sense.

meet: reasonable, just

diarrhea: possibly dysentery

Hyrcania: see **Lesson Fifteen**

chaste and continent: well-behaved, self-controlled

People

Hephaestion, Craterus: see introductory notes

Historic Occasions

327 B.C.: Alexander married Roxane

Reading

Part One

Departing thence, he entered into the country of **Parthia** [where, not having much to do], he began to **apparel himself after the fashion of the barbarous people,** because he thought thereby the better to win the hearts of the countrymen, framing himself unto their own fashions: or else to try the hearts of the Macedonians, to see how they would like the manner of the Persians (which he meant to bring them unto) in reverencing of him as they [the Persians] did their king, by little and little acquainting them to allow the alteration and change of his life.

This notwithstanding, he would not at the first take up the apparel of the **Medes**, which was very **strange** and altogether barbarous. [He adopted neither the trousers nor the **sleeved vest**, nor the **tiara** for the head, but taking a middle way between the **Persian mode and the Macedonian**, so contrived his habit that it was not so flaunting as the one, and yet more pompous and magnificent than the other.] At the first he did not wear it but when he would talk with the barbarous people, or else privately amongst his friends and familiars. Afterwards, notwithstanding, he shewed himself openly to the people in that apparel when he gave them audience. This sight grieved the Macedonians much: but they had his virtues in such admiration, that they thought it **meet** in some things he should take his own pleasure, since he had been often hurt in the wars, and not long before had his leg broken with an arrow, and another time, had such a blow with a stone full in his neck [which dimmed his sight for a good while afterwards. And yet all this could not hinder him from exposing himself freely to any dangers, insomuch that he passed **the river Orexartes**, which he took to be the Tanais; and putting the Scythians to flight, followed them above a hundred furlongs, though suffering all the time from a **diarrhea**.]

[*omission for length*]

Furthermore, Alexander, fearing that the Macedonians being weary with this long war, would go no further; he left all the rest of his army behind, and took only twenty thousand footmen and three thousand horsemen of the choicest men of his army, and with them invaded the country of **Hyrcania.** There he made an oration unto [these soldiers]; and told them that the barbarous people of Asia had but seen them as it were in a dream, and if they should now return back into Macedon, having but only stirred them, and not altogether subdued Asia: the people, offended with them, would set upon them as they went home [*short omission*].

Nevertheless, he gave any man leave to return that would, [merely] protesting therewith against them that would go, how they did forsake him, his friends, and those who had so good hearts towards him, as to follow him in so noble a journey, to conquer the whole earth [for] the Macedonians. This matter is reported thus in a letter which Alexander wrote unto Antipater: and there he writeth furthermore, that having made this oration unto them, they all cried out, and bade him lead them into what part of the world he would. When they had granted their good wills, it was no hard matter afterwards, to win the rest of the common sort [of soldiers] who followed the example of the chiefest.

Thereupon he did frame himself the more to live after the fashion of the country there, and also to bring the men of that country unto the manner of the Macedonians: being persuaded, that by this mixture and interchange of manners one with another, he should by friendship, more than force, make them agree lovingly together when [the time came] that he should be so far from the country of Persia. For this purpose, therefore, he chose thirty thousand of their children of that country, and set them to learn the Greek tongue, and to be brought up in the discipline of wars, after the Macedonian manner: and gave them schoolmasters and captains to train them in each faculty.

Part Two

And for the marrying of Roxane: he fancied her, seeing her at a feast where he was; which fell out as well for his turn, as if he had with better advice and counsel loved her. For the barbarous people were very proud of this match when they saw him make alliance with them in this sort, insomuch as they loved him better then they did before, because they saw in those things he was always so **chaste and continent**, that, notwithstanding, he was marvellously in love with her; yet he would not dishonourably touch this young lady before he was married unto her.

[Noticing, also, that among his chief friends and favourites, **Hephaestion** most approved of all he did and complied with and imitated him in his change of habits; while **Craterus** continued strict in the observation of the customs and fashions of his own country; he made it his practice to employ the first in all transactions with the Persians, and the latter when he had to do with the Greeks or Macedonians. In general he showed more affection for **Hephaestion** [but] more respect for **Craterus**; **Hephaestion**, as he used to say, being Alexander's, and **Craterus** the king's friend.]

Hereupon these two persons bare one another grudge in their hearts, and oftentimes brake out in open quarrel: insomuch as on a time being in India, they drew their swords and fought together, and divers of their friends ran to take part with either side. Thither came Alexander himself also, who openly before them all, bitterly took up **Hephaestion**, and called him fool and bedlam [*short omission*]. Privately also, he sharply rebuked **Craterus**, and calling them both before him, he made them friends together, swearing by Jupiter Ammon, and by all the other gods, that he loved them two of all men living, nevertheless if ever he found that they fell out together again, they should both die for it, or him at the least that first began to quarrel. So ever after that, they say, there was never foul word nor deed between them, not so much as in sport only.

[*material omitted between these lessons*]

Narration and Discussion

One reason Alexander changed his dress was "to see how [his people] would like the manner of the Persians (which he meant to bring them unto) in reverencing of him as they did their king, by little and little acquainting them to allow the alteration and change of his life." Do you agree that the language of clothes is important? How might what we wear affect our relationships with others?

How did Alexander stem the quarrel between his best friends?

For older students: Alexander's change in appearance seems to have also changed his self-image. How might this affect his future decisions?

Lesson Seventeen
Introduction

There is a lengthy omission between **Lessons Sixteen and Seventeen**, involving intrigue and misconduct in Alexander's court. It includes the execution of Philotas, the son of Parmenio; and then of Parmenio himself, an old friend who had served under King Philip. All this made Alexander's friends increasingly frightened of his cruelty.

This lesson builds on the climate of mistrust sparked by those events. It describes the murder of Clitus, an act that would haunt Alexander for the rest of his life (see **Lesson Three**).

Vocabulary

>**not of set purpose:** not premeditated
>
>**wethers:** castrated male sheep (used for sacrificial purposes)
>
>**churlish:** mean-spirited, rude
>
>**Spithridates' sword:** referring to the Battle of Granicus

"Do you not think," said he…: Alexander's reason for saying this is not clear; but it may have been the fact that Alexander did not respond directly to his accusations which further enraged Clitus.

Persian girdle and long white garment: belt and tunic, described in **Lesson Sixteen**

rehearsed: recited

partisan: spear

prognostication: prediction

near friend of Aristotle: possibly the great-nephew of Aristotle

despising and slighting: thinking little of

censure and reproach: criticism, condemnation

audacious: bold

insinuate himself: inch or "worm" himself

austerity: stern manner

People

Philotas: the son of Parmenio

Clitus (Cleitus): "Clitus the Black" had saved Alexander's life at the Battle of the Granicus (**Lesson Four**).

Castor and Pollux: immortal brothers believed to be the patrons of travellers and sailors (giving them fair winds)

Callisthenes: a Greek historian, and a close friend or relative of Aristotle, who accompanied Alexander on his journey. He had also been the tutor of **Hermolaus** (**Lesson Eighteen**).

Anaxarchus: a philosopher

Alexander

Historic Occasions

328 B.C.: the death of **Clitus**

Reading

Part One

Not long after that followed the murder of Clitus, the which, to hear it simply told, would seem much more cruel than the death of Philotas. But reporting the cause and the time together in which it chanced, it will be found that it was **not of set purpose**, but by chance, and unfortunately, that Alexander being overcome with wine, did unluckily wreak his anger upon Clitus.

The manner of his misfortune was this: there came certain men of the low countries from the seaside, that brought apples of Greece [Dryden: *Grecian fruit*] unto Alexander. Alexander wondering to see them so green and fair, sent for Clitus to show him them, and to give him some of them. Clitus by chance did sacrifice at that time unto the gods, and left his sacrifice to go unto Alexander: howbeit there were three **wethers** that followed him, on whom the accustomed sprinklings had been done already to have sacrificed them. Alexander understanding that, told it to his soothsayers, Aristander and Cleomantis Laconian, who both did answer him that it was an ill sign. Alexander thereupon gave order straight that they should do sacrifice for the health of Clitus, and specially for that three days before he dreamed one night that he saw Clitus in a mourning gown, sitting amongst the sons of Parmenio, the which were all dead before.

This notwithstanding, Clitus did not make an end of his sacrifice, but came straight to supper to the king, who had that day sacrificed unto Castor and Pollux. [And when they had drunk pretty hard, some of the company fell a-singing the verses of one Pranichus, or as others say, of Pierion], against certain captains of the Macedonians, which had not long before been overcome by the barbarous people, and only to shame them and to make the company laugh.

With these verses, ancient men that were at this feast became much offended, and grew angry with the poet that made them, and the minstrel that sang them. Alexander, on the other side, and his familiars, liked them very well, and commanded the minstrel to sing still. Clitus, therewith, all being overtaken with wine, and besides of a **churlish** nature, proud and arrogant, fell into greater choler, and said that it was neither well nor honestly done in that sort to speak ill of those poor Macedonian captains (and specially amongst the barbarous people their enemies), which were far better men than they that laughed them to scorn, although their fortune [was] much worse than theirs. Alexander then replied, and said that, saying so, he [Clitus] pleaded for himself, calling cowardliness "misfortune."

Then Clitus standing up, said again:

> "But yet this my 'cowardliness' saved thy life, that callest thyself the son of the gods, when thou turnedst thy back from Spithridates' sword; and the blood which these poor Macedonians did shed for thee, and the wounds which they received of their bodies fighting for thee, have made thee so great, that thou disdainest now to have King Philip for thy father, and wilt needs make thyself the son of Jupiter Ammon."

Alexander being moved with these words, straight replied: "O villain, thinkest thou to escape unpunished for these proud words of thine, which thou usest continually against me, making the Macedonians rebel against Alexander?"

Clitus answered again, "Too much are we punished, Alexander, for our pains and service to receive such reward: nay, most happy think we them that long since are dead and gone, not now to see the Macedonians scourged with rods of the Medes and compelled to curry favour with the Persians to have access unto [the] king."

Thus, Clitus boldly speaking against Alexander, and Alexander again answering and reviling him: the gravest men sought to pacify this stir and tumult. Alexander then turning himself unto Xenodochus [the] Cardian and Artemius [the] Colophonian: **"Do you not think,"** said **he, "that the Grecians are amongst the Macedonians, as demigods that walk among brute beasts?"**

Clitus for all this would not give over his impudency and malapertness, but cried out, and bade Alexander speak openly what he had to say, or else not to bid free men come to sup with him that were wont to speak frankly: if not, to keep with the barbarous slaves that

Alexander

honoured his **Persian girdle and long white garment**.

Then could Alexander no longer hold his choler, but took an apple that was upon his table, and threw it at Clitus; and looked for his sword, the which Aristophanes, one of his guard that waited on him, had of purpose taken from him. And when every man came straight about him to stay him, and to pray him to be contented: he immediately rose from the board and called his guard unto him in the Macedonian tongue (which was a sign of great trouble to follow after it) and commanded a trumpeter to sound the alarm. But he, drawing back, would not sound: whereupon Alexander struck him with his fist. Notwithstanding, the trumpeter was greatly commended afterwards [for disobeying an order which would have put the whole army into tumult and confusion].

All this could not quiet Clitus, whereupon his friends with much ado thrust him out of the hall: but he came in again at another door, and arrogantly and unreverently **rehearsed** this verse of the poet Euripides, out of *Andromache*'s tragedy:

[In Greece, alas! How ill things ordered are!]

Then Alexander taking a **partisan** from one of his guard, as Clitus was coming towards him, and had lift[ed] up the hanging before the door, he ran him through the body, so that Clitus fell to the ground, and fetching one groan, died presently.

Part Two

Alexander's choler had left him straight, and he became marvellous sorrowful: and when he saw his friends round about him say never a word, he plucked the **partisan** out of his [Clitus'] body, and would have thrust it into his own throat. Howbeit his guard about him caught him by the hands and carried him perforce into his chamber: and there he did nothing all that night but weep bitterly, and the next day following, until such time as he was able to cry no more, but lying on the ground, only lay sighing.

His friends hearing his voice no more, were afraid, and came into his chamber by force to comfort him. But Alexander would hear none of them, saving Aristander the soothsayer, who remembered him of his dream he had of Clitus before, which was a **prognostication** of that which had happened: whereby it appeared that it was his destiny before he was born. This seemed to comfort Alexander.

[They now brought **Callisthenes** the philosopher (the **near friend of Aristotle**) and **Anaxarchus** of Abdera to him. Callisthenes used moral language, and gentle and soothing means, hoping to find access for words of reason, and get ahold upon the passion. But Anaxarchus, who had always taken a course of his own in philosophy, and had a name for **despising and slighting** his contemporaries, as soon as he came in cried out aloud,

> "Is this the Alexander whom the whole world looks to, lying here weeping like a slave for fear of the **censure and reproach** of men, to whom he himself ought to be a law and measure of equity, if he would use the right his conquests have given him as supreme lord and governor of all, and not be the victim of a vain and idle opinion? Do you not know," said he, "that Jupiter is represented to have Justice and Law on each hand of him, to signify that all the actions of a conqueror are lawful and just?"

With these and the like speeches, Anaxarchus indeed allayed the king's grief, but withal corrupted his character, rendering him more **audacious** and lawless than he had been. Nor did he fail by these means to **insinuate** himself into his favour, and to make Callisthenes' company, which at all times because of his **austerity** was not very acceptable, more uneasy and disagreeable to him.]

Narration and Discussion

Had Alexander lost his principles (such as devotion to his friends), or was this simply an unfortunate event caused by too much drink?

How did the words of Anaxarchus soothe away the king's guilt, but also "corrupt his character?" Can you think of real-life or literary examples where facing an uncomfortable truth has led to repentance? (A Bible verse to look up: Proverbs 28:23.)

Alexander

Lesson Eighteen

Introduction

The last lesson told the story of Clitus, Alexander's old friend who was killed as a result both of his own temper and the king's increasingly unstable nature. Now we read about another man who paid a similar price, but this time for his unwillingness to compromise his deepest principles.

Vocabulary

    touching the seasons…: talking about the weather

    galled Anaxarchus to the quick: stung him to the heart

    contented with his own: he was happy with what he had

    commendation: praise

    nosegays and flowers: bouquets of flowers

    Hermolaus' conspiracy: Alexander's page Hermolaus conspired with others to assassinate the king, in revenge for a certain punishment. Hermolaus blamed **Callisthenes** for suggesting the idea.

    engaged in the design: involved in the conspiracy

    the murderers into their cities…: this seems to refer to any who would conspire against him

    brought up with him: brought up in Aristotle's house

    kinsman: relative

    apprehended: arrested, seized

People

    Callisthenes, Anaxarchus: see previous notes

    Craterus: see introductory notes

Historic Occasions

327 B.C.: the conspiracy of Hermolaus, while the army was in Bactria

Reading

Part One

It is written also that there was certain talk one night at King Alexander's board **touching the seasons of the year, and temperateness of the air**, and that **Callisthenes** was of the opinion which maintained that the country they were in at that time was much colder, and the winter also sharper, than in Greece. **Anaxarchus** held the contrary opinion, and stiffly maintained it, insomuch as Callisthenes said unto him: "And yet must thou grant, that it is colder here than there. [For there you used to have but one threadbare cloak to keep out the coldest winter, and here you have three good warm mantles one over another."]

This **galled Anaxarchus to the quick** and made him more angry than before; and for the other rhetoricians and flatterers, they did also hate him [Callisthenes], because they saw him followed [by] young men for his eloquence, and beloved also of old men for his honest life, the which was very grave, modest, and **contented with his own**, desiring no man's else. Whereby men found that the reason he alleged for following of Alexander in this voyage was true: for he said that he came to be a humble suitor to the king, to restore his banished citizens into their country again, and to replenish their city with inhabitants.

Now, though [Callisthenes'] estimation made him chiefly to be envied; yet did he himself give his enemies occasion to accuse him. For oftentimes being invited by the king to supper, either he would not come, or if he came, he would be mute, and say nothing, showing by his gravity and silence that nothing pleased him that was either said or done. Whereupon Alexander [him]self said on a time unto him:

I can not think that person wise,

That in his own case hath no eyes.

It is reported of [Callisthenes] also, that being at supper on a time with the king, divers requesting him to make an oration on the sudden in

commendation of the Macedonians: he made such an eloquent oration upon that matter, that all they that heard him rose from the board, and clapping their hands for joy, cast **nosegays and flowers** upon him. But yet Alexander at that time said unto him that which the poet Euripides said:

> It is no mastery to be eloquent,
>
> In handling of a plenteous argument.

["Therefore," said he, "if you will show the force of your eloquence, tell my Macedonians their faults, and dispraise them, that by hearing their errors they may learn to be better for the future." Callisthenes presently obeyed him, retracting all he had said before by] declaring that the [earlier] dissension amongst the Grecians [had increased] **King Philip's** power, alleging these verses:

> Where discord reigns in realm or town,
>
> Even wicked folk do win renown.

But by this occasion, he purchased himself great ill-will of the Macedonians.

[*omission for length*]

Part Two

[Therefore when **Hermolaus' conspiracy** came to be discovered, the charges which [Callisthenes'] enemies brought against him were the more easily believed, particularly that when the young man asked him what he should do to be the most illustrious person on earth, he told him the readiest way was to kill him who was already so; and that to incite him to commit the deed, he bade him not be awed by the golden couch, but remember Alexander was a man equally infirm and vulnerable as another. However, none of Hermolaus' accomplices, in the utmost extremity, made any mention of Callisthenes' being **engaged in the design**.] And Alexander himself also writing of this treason immediately after, unto **Craterus**, Attalus, and Alcetas, said that their servants which had been racked and put to the torture did constantly affirm that they only had conspired his death, and no man else was privy unto it.

But afterwards, he sent another letter unto Antipater, wherein he directly accused Callisthenes, and said that his servants [Dryden: *the young men*] had already been stoned to death by the Macedonians; howbeit that he himself would afterwards also punish the master, and those that had sent unto him and that had received **the murderers into their cities, who came of purpose to kill him**. And therein he plainly shewed the ill-will he bare unto Aristotle, for that Callisthenes had been **brought up with him**, being his **kinsman**.

[Callisthenes' death is variously related. Some say he was hanged by Alexander's orders; others, that he died of sickness in prison; but Chares writes he was kept in chains seven months after he was **apprehended**, on purpose that he might be proceeded against in full council, when Aristotle should be present; and that growing very fat, and contracting a disease of vermin, he there died about the time that Alexander was wounded in India, in the country of the Malli Oxydracae; all (of) which came to pass afterwards.]

[*omission for length*]

Narration and Discussion

Why did Anaxarchus and his followers resent Callisthenes?

Was Callisthenes wise or foolish in obeying Alexander's order to "dispraise" the Macedonians? What was the result? What would you have done in his situation?

Lesson Nineteen

Introduction

Alexander's journey to India grew out of his desire to completely conquer the known world. From a historical standpoint, we run into some limitations and difficulties with Plutarch's version of the story. One problem is that other authors, such as Arrian in his *Anabasis*, covered the Indian campaign in more detail than Plutarch did. Another is that later historians have re-examined the earlier accounts, trying to determine what details were most likely true, and which ones may have been exaggerated or simply misunderstood. One example is Alexander's granting of kingdoms to Porus in **Lesson Twenty**; in fact, Porus probably ruled that territory already.

For the purposes of this study, we will confine ourselves to the story as the "moral biographer" Plutarch tells it. But those who wish to go deeper will find no shortage of material!

Vocabulary

unwildsom: unwieldy, awkward

carriage: literally, the things to be carried

deliberation: planning

rigorous: Dryden says "severe"

a stronghold which Sisimethres kept/the city of Nysa: these places are not in India, and the stories happened at other times; they are included to show Alexander's character

than all Egypt: probably an exaggeration

capitulation: giving in, surrender

the choice of his horsemen: his best horsemen

leave: hesitate

the twain: the two possibilities

scantly: scarcely

four cubits and a span high: about seven feet tall

People

Taxiles: the ruler of a region in the Punjab (in present-day Pakistan), of which the capital city was Taxila. His proper name was Ambhi, but the Greek chroniclers called him Taxiles/Taxilas. He took part in the **Battle of the Hydaspes**, and was involved first in pursuit of and then in negotiations with **Porus**. He continued to govern a large territory after the death of Alexander.

Porus [Poros]: the ruler of a neighbouring region, who was not on good terms with Taxiles.

Historic Occasions

Winter of 328/327 B.C.: the assault on Sisimethres' fortress

326 B.C.: the battle of the **Hydaspes River,** against Porus

On the Map

Referring to a map of Alexander's journeys in India will be helpful.

Reading

Part One

Alexander being ready to take his journey to go conquer India, perceiving that his army was very heavy and **unwildsom** to remove, for the wonderful **carriage** and spoils they had with them: the carts one morning being laden, he first burnt his own **carriage**, and next his friends', and then commanded that they should also set the carriage of the Macedonians afire. [This was an act which in the **deliberation** of it had seemed more dangerous and difficult than it proved in the execution.] For there [were] very few of them that were angry therewith, and the most part of them (as if they had been secretly moved by some god) with loud cries of joy, one of them gave unto another such necessary things as they had need of, and afterwards of themselves did burn and spoil all the rest. [The sight of (this) redoubled Alexander's zeal and eagerness for his design. And, indeed,] this made Alexander much more **rigorous** than he was before, besides that he was already become cruel enough; and without mercy or pardon [he] did sharply punish every man that offended. For having commanded Menander, one of his friends, to keep him a [fortress], he put him to death, because he would not remain there. Furthermore, he himself slew Orsodates (a captain of the barbarous people) with a dart, for that

Alexander

he rebelled against him.

[*omission: certain signs and omens*]

And truly so did he sustain many dangers in those wars and was oftentimes hurt in fight. But the greatest loss he had of his men was for lack of victuals, and by the infection of the air. For he, striving to overcome fortune by valiantness, and her force by virtue, thought nothing impossible for a valiant man, neither anything able to withstand a noble heart.

It is reported, that when he went to besiege **a stronghold which Sisimethres kept**, being thought [unassaultable], and that his soldiers were in despair of it, he asked one Oxyarthes what heart Sisimethres had. Oxyarthes answered him, that he was the veriest coward in the world. "O, that is well," quoth Alexander: "then it is to be won, if that be true thou sayest, since the captain of the [fortress] is but a coward." So he took it of a sudden, by putting Sisimethres in a great fear. After that also, he did besiege another [fortress] of as great strength and difficulty to assault as the other, and making the young soldiers of the Macedonians to go to the assault, he called one of them unto him, whose name also was Alexander, unto whom he said thus: "Alexander, this day thou must fight like a man, and it be but for thy namesake." The young man did not forget his words, for he fought so valiantly, that he was slain, for whom Alexander was very sorry.

Another time when his men were afraid, and durst not come near unto the **city of Nysa** to assault it, because there ran a very deep river hard by the walls: he came to the riverside, and said: "Oh, what a coward am I, that never learned to swim!" and so prepared himself to swim over upon his shield. [Here, after the assault was over, the ambassadors who, from several towns which he had blocked up, came to submit to him and make their peace, were surprised to find him still in his armour, without anyone in waiting or attendance upon him; and when at last someone brought him a cushion, he made the eldest of them, named Acuphis, take it and sit down upon it.]

Acuphis marvelling at Alexander's great courtesy, asked him what they should do for him, thenceforth to be his good friends. "I will," said Alexander, "that they from whom thou comest as ambassador unto us do make thee their king: and withal that they do send me a hundred of their best men for hostages." Acuphis, smiling, answered him again: "But I shall rule them better, king, if I send you the worst, and not the best."

Part Two

There was a king called **Taxiles**, a very wise man, who had a great country in India, no less in bigness and circuit **than all Egypt**, and as full of good pasture and fruits as any country in the world could be: who came on a time to salute Alexander, and said unto him:

> "What should we need, Alexander, to fight, and make wars one with another, if thou comest not to take away our water, and our necessary commodity to live by: for which things, men of judgment must needs fight? As for other goods, if I be richer than thou, I am ready to give thee of mine: and if I have less, I will not think scorn to thank thee, if thou wilt give me some of thine."

Alexander [*omission*] embraced him, and said unto him:

> "Thinkest thou this meeting of ours can be without fight, for all these goodly fair words? No, no, thou hast won nothing by that: for I will fight and contend with thee in honesty and courtesy, because thou shalt not exceed me in bounty and liberality."

So Alexander taking divers gifts of him, but giving more unto Taxiles: he drank to him one night at supper, and said, "I drink to thee a thousand talents in gold." This gift misliked Alexander's friends: but in recompense thereof, he won the hearts of many of those barbarous lords and princes of that country.

[*short omission*]

But the grave philosophers and wise men of India did greatly trouble him. For they reproved the kings and princes of the Indians for that they yielded unto Alexander, and [they] procured the free cities to take arms against him. [He took several of these also and caused them to be hanged.]

Part Three

Learning suggestion for Part Three: *You may find it helpful to use figures or small objects to show the events of the battle as you read.*

For **King Porus**, Alexander himself writeth in his epistles all his acts at large which he did against him. For he sayeth that, both their camps lying on either side of the **River of Hydaspes**, King Porus set his elephants upon the bank of the river with their heads towards their enemies, to keep them from passing over: and that he himself [Alexander] did continually make a noise and tumult in his camp, to acquaint his men not to be afraid of the barbarous people.

Furthermore, that in a dark night when there was no moonlight, he took part of his footmen, and **the choice of his horsemen**, and went far from his enemies to get over into a little island. When he was come into the island, there fell a wonderful shower of rain, great winds, lightnings and thunders upon his camp, insomuch as he saw many of his men burnt by lightning in this little island. This notwithstanding, he did not **leave** to get over to the other side of the river.

The river being swollen with the great flood of rain that fell the night before, overflowing the banks, it did eat into the ground where the water ran: so that Alexander when he had passed over the river, and was come to the other side, found himself in very ill case, for that he could hardly keep his feet, because the earth was very slippery under him, and the rage of the water had eaten into it, and broke[n] it down on every side. It is written of him, that then he said unto the Athenians, "[O ye Athenians, will ye believe what dangers I incur to merit your praise?]" Thus Onesicritus reporteth it.

[Alexander says (that) here the men left their boats, and passed the breach in their armour, up to the breast in water, and that then he advanced with his horse about twenty furlongs before his foot [soldiers], concluding that if the enemy charged him with their cavalry, he should be too strong for them; [and] if with their foot [soldiers], his own would come up (in) time enough to his assistance.]

One of **the twain** fell out as he had guessed. For a thousand horsemen, and three score chariots armed with his enemies, gave him charge before their great company, whom he overthrew, and took all their chariots, and slew four hundred of the men-of-arms in the field.

King Porus then knowing by those signs that Alexander was there in person, and [that he] had passed over the river: he marched towards him with all his army in battle array, saving a few which he left behind to resist the Macedonians, if they shewed force to pass over the river.

Alexander, being afraid of the great multitude of his enemies, and of the terror of the elephants, did not give charge upon the midst of the battle; but being himself in the left wing, [he] gave charge upon the corner of the enemy's left wing, and [he] also commanded them that were in the right wing to do the like. So, both the ends of the enemy's army were broken and put to flight; and they that fled ran unto the elephants and gathered themselves together about them.

Thus, the battle being begun, the conflict continued long, insomuch as the enemies were **scantly** all overthrown by three of the clock in the afternoon. [Almost all the historians agree in relating that Porus was **four cubits and a span high**, and that when he was upon his elephant, which was of the largest size, his stature and bulk were so answerable, that he appeared to be proportionably mounted, as a horseman on his horse.] This elephant did shew great wit and care, to save the king his master. For whilst he perceived his master was strong enough, he lustily repulsed those which came to assail him: but when he found that he began to faint, having many wounds upon his body, and arrows sticking in it: then being afraid lest his master should fall down from his back, he softly fell on his knees, and gently taking his darts and arrows with his trunk, which he had in his body, he plucked them all from him one after another.

Narration and Discussion

Tell about the battle Alexander fought with Porus.

"For he, striving to overcome fortune by valiantness, and her force by virtue, thought nothing impossible for a valiant man, neither anything able to withstand a noble heart." Do you agree?

Alexander

Lesson Twenty

Introduction

After the victorious but costly battle at Hydaspes, Alexander wanted to continue the campaign, and to cross the Ganges River. However, his men refused to go on, either from homesickness and exhaustion, or from embarrassment that they had had so much difficulty fighting a minor ruler like Porus. Alexander was forced to agree to head back.

Vocabulary

satrap: governor

brought up of a whelp: brought up from a puppy

veneration: awe, reverence

rampart: defensive wall

cuirass: a piece of chest armour

the method of his cure: a course of treatment by his physicians

scimitar: curved sword

half in a swound: half unconscious

On the Map

From the River Hydaspes, Alexander's troops continued to the southwest, following the Indus river to the Arabian Sea.

Reading

Part One

Porus being taken, Alexander asked him how he should handle him. "Princely," answered Porus. [Dryden: *"As a king."*] Alexander asked him again, if he would say anything else. "I comprehend all," said he, "in this word 'princely.'" [And Alexander, accordingly, not only suffered him to govern his own kingdom as **satrap** under himself, but [he] gave him also the additional territory of various independent tribes whom he subdued, a district which, it is said, contained fifteen several nations and five thousand considerable towns, besides abundance of villages. To another government, three times as large as this, he appointed Philip, one of his friends.]

His horse Bucephalus died at this battle, not in the field, but afterwards whilst he was in cure for the wounds he had on his body: but as Onesicritus saith, he died even worn for very age. Alexander was as sorry for his death as if he had lost any of his familiar friends; and for proof thereof, he built a great city in the place where his horse was buried, upon the river of Hydaspes, the which he called after his name, Bucephalusia. It is reported also, that having lost a dog of his called Peritas, which he had **brought up of a whelp**, and loved very dearly: he built also a city and called it after his name. [So Sotion assures us he was informed by Potamon of Lesbos].

This last battle against King Porus killed the Macedonians' hearts, and made them that they had no desire to go any further to conquer India.

[*omission for length*]

Alexander, offended with his men's refusal, kept close in his tent for certain days, and lay upon the ground, saying that he did not thank them for all that they had done [already], unless they passed over the River of Ganges also: and that to return back again, it was as much as to confess that he had been overcome. At the length, when he saw and considered that there was great reason in his friends' persuasions which laboured to comfort him, and that his soldiers came to the door of his tent, crying and lamenting, humbly beseeching him to lead them back again: in the end he took pity of them, and was contented to return.

This notwithstanding, before he departed from those parts, he put forth many vain and false devices to make his name immortal among that people. He made armours of greater proportion than his own, and mangers for horses, higher then the common sort: moreover, he made bits [of bridles] also far heavier then the common sort and made them to be thrown and scattered abroad in every place. He built great altars also in honour of the gods, the which the kings of the Praesians have in great **veneration** at this day: and passing over the river, do make sacrifices there, after the manner of the Grecians.

[*omission for length*]

Part Two

[Alexander was now eager to see the ocean. To which purpose he caused a great many rowboats and rafts to be built], in the which he easily went down the rivers at his pleasure. Howbeit, this his pleasant going by water was not without war: for he would land oftentimes, and did assail cities, and conquered all as he went. Yet in assailing the city of [the] Mallians (which they say are the warlikest men of all the Indians), he was almost slain there.

For, having repulsed the enemies from the wall, he himself was the first man that set foot on a ladder to get up, the which brake as soon as ever he was gotten upon the **rampart**. Then the barbarous people coming together against the wall, did throw [darts] at him from beneath, and many time[s] lighted upon him. Alexander, having few of his men about him, made no more ado but leaped down from the wall in the midst of his enemies, and by good hap lighted on his feet. His harness making a great noise with the fall, the barbarous people were afraid, thinking they had seen some light or spirit go before him: so that at the first they all betook them to their legs, and ran scatteringly here and there.

But after that, when they came again to themselves, and saw that he had but two gentlemen only about him, they came and set upon him of all hands, and fought with him at the sword or push of the pike, and so hurt him very sore through his armour: but one among the rest, being somewhat further off, gave him such a terrible blow with an arrow, that he struck him through his **cuirass**, and shot him in at the side under his breast. The blow entered so into his body, that he fell down on one of his knees. Whereupon, he that had stricken him with his arrow ran suddenly to him with a **scimitar** drawn in his hand. Howbeit Peucestas and Limnaeus stepped before him, and were both hurt: Limnaeus was slain presently, and Peucestas fought it out, till at the length, Alexander himself slew the barbarous man with his own hand, after he had many grievous wounds upon his body. At the length he had a blow with a dart on his neck that so astonished him, that he leaned against the wall looking upon his enemies.

In the meantime, the Macedonians compassing him round about, took him and carried him into his tent **half in a swound**, and past knowledge: whereupon there ran a rumour straight in the camp that Alexander was dead. They had much ado to cut the arrow asunder that was of wood: so his **cuirass** being plucked off with great pain, yet were they to pluck the arrowhead out of his body, which stuck in one of his bones: the which as it is reported, was four fingers long, and three fingers broad. [During the operation, he was taken with almost mortal swoonings, but when it was out he came to himself again. Yet though all danger was past, he continued very weak, and confined himself a great while to a regular diet and **the method of his cure**]: until he heard the Macedonians cry, and make great noise about his tent, desirous to see him. Then he [took his cloak] and came out amongst them all: and after he had done sacrifice unto the gods for recovery of his health, he went on his journey again, and in the same did conquer many great countries and took divers goodly cities.

Narration and Discussion

"…he put forth many vain and false devices to make his name immortal among that people." How did Alexander himself contribute to romantic legends about his greatness?

What may have been some of the reasons that Alexander was less successful in India than he had been elsewhere?

Lesson Twenty-One

Introduction

Part One of this lesson is a dialogue about philosophical conundrums. Those working in groups might enjoy acting it out.

Vocabulary

pertinent: this can be translated "correct"

sea Oceanum: This is a translation of the Latin "Mare Oceanum" or "World-Encircling Ocean." It referred to exactly that: the Atlantic Ocean, which surrounded the known world.

going still through the country: as explained in the next sentence, they created a "travelling banquet"

rising up of height: the meaning of this is not clear

fooling: dancing, drinking, and revelry

Historic Occasions

324 B.C.: Alexander returned to Persia

On the Map

Beginning the journey back to Macedonia, the army moved westward, following the Arabian Sea coast. They then travelled northwest through the countries of **Gedrosia** and **Carmania**.

Reading

Part One

[In this voyage, (Alexander) took ten Indian philosophers prisoner, who had been most active in persuading Sabbas to revolt [in 325 B.C.], and who had caused the Macedonians a great deal of trouble. These men, called Gymnosophists, were reputed to be extremely ready and succinct in their answers, which he made trial of by putting difficult questions to them, letting them know that those whose answers were not **pertinent** should be put to death; of which he made the eldest of them judge.]

The question he asked the first man was this:

1. Whether the dead or the living were the greater number. He answered, the living. "For the dead," said he, "are no more men."

2. The second man he asked: whether the earth, or the sea brought forth most creatures. He answered, the earth. "For the sea," said he, "is but a part of the earth."

3. To the third man: which of all beasts was the subtlest. "That," said he, "which man hitherto never knew."

4. To the fourth: why did he make Sabbas rebel? "Because," said he, "he should live honourably, or die vilely."

5. To the fifth, which he thought was first, the day, or the night? He answered, "the day, by a day." The king, finding his answer strange, added to this speech: "Strange questions must needs have strange answers."

6. Coming to the sixth man, he asked him how a man should come to be beloved. "If he be a good man," said he, "not terrible."

7. To the seventh, how a man should be a god? "In doing a thing," said he, "impossible for a man."

8. To the eight, which was the stronger: life or death? "Life," said he, "that suffereth so many troubles."

9. And unto the ninth and last man: how long a man should live? "Until," said he, "he think it better to die, than to live."

When Alexander had heard these answers, he turned unto the judge, and bade him give his judgment upon them. The judge said [that] they had all answered one worse than another.

"Then shalt thou die first," said Alexander, "because thou hast given such sentence."

["Not so, O King," replied the gymnosophist, "unless you said falsely that he should die first who made the worst answer."

In conclusion Alexander gave them presents and dismissed them.]

[*omission for length*]

Part Two

Alexander continued seven months travelling upon the rivers, to go see the great **sea Oceanum**. Then he took ship, and sailed into a little island called Scillustis, howbeit others call it Psiltucis. There he landed, made sacrifices unto the gods, and viewed the greatness and nature of the sea Oceanum, and all the situation of the coast upon that sea, as far as he could go.

[*omission for length: some difficult travels*]

After sixty days' march he came into **Gedrosia**, where he found great plenty of all things, which the neighbouring kings and governors of provinces, hearing of his approach, had taken care to provide.] After he had refreshed his army there a little, he went through the country of **Carmania**, where he continued seven days together banqueting, **going still through the country**. For night and day, he was feasting continually with his friends upon a [platform erected on a] scaffold longer than broad, **rising up of height**, and drawn with eight goodly horse[s]. After that scaffold followed divers other chariots covered over, [some covered with purple and embroidered canopies, and some with green boughs, which were continually supplied afresh]: and in those were Alexander's other friends and captains with garlands of flowers upon their heads, which drank and made merry together. [Here was now no] helmet, pike, dart, nor target seen: but gold and silver bowls, cups, and flagons in the soldiers' hands, all the way as they went, drawing wine out of great pipes and vessels which they carried with them, one drinking to another, some marching in the fields going forward, and others also set at the table. About them were the minstrels playing and piping on their flutes and shawms, and women singing and dancing, and **fooling** by the way as they went.

[*omission: mature content*]

Narration and Discussion

In Part One, which was your favourite answer of the nine?

How did the tenth philosopher show that he was the wisest of all?

Lesson Twenty-Two

Introduction

Alexander, in spite of the travelling party described in the previous lesson, had suffered setbacks during his time in India. Many men had died, and the army was in such a weak state that cities he had "conquered" were rebelling. People in Macedonia thought (happily or sadly) that he would never return from his journey. But Alexander was not ready to give up the territory he had claimed, or his dream of a triumphant return. He even took the opportunity to get married.

Vocabulary

>**the narrative of his voyage:** see the notes in "On the Map"
>
>**he resolved himself to sail…:** this voyage was planned, but did not take place
>
>**great insolencies…:** the governors were growing rich by overtaxing their people
>
>**broil and sedition:** turmoil, uprisings
>
>**a faction against Antipater:** Antipater had been left to govern during Alexander's absence
>
>**a crown:** a piece of gold

People

>**Cyrus, king of Persia:** Cyrus the Great, who lived in the sixth century B.C., was the founder of the Persian empire.

Alexander

Antigonus with one eye: a Macedonian general; see introductory notes

Historic Occasions

324 B.C.: Alexander returned to Persia and married Statira

On the Map

As this is a return journey, most of the places have been mentioned in previous lessons.

Reading

Part One

[At Gedrosia, Aleander's admiral, Nearchus, came to him and delighted him so with **the narrative of his voyage**, that **he resolved himself to sail** out of the mouth of [the] Euphrates with a great fleet, with which he designed to go round by Arabia and Africa, and so by Hercules' Pillars into the Mediterranean; in order for which he directed all sorts of vessels to be built at Thapsacus, and made provision everywhere of seamen and pilots.]

But now the difficulty of the journey which he took upon him for the conquest of India, the danger he was in when he fought with the Mallians, and the number of his men which he lost besides which was very great; all these things considered together [made] men believe that he should never return with safety. They made all the people (which he had conquered) bold to rise against him and gave his governors and lieutenants of provinces occasion to commit **great insolencies, robberies, and exactions** of people. To be short, it put all his kingdom in **broil and sedition**. [Even at home, Olympias and Cleopatra had raised **a faction against Antipater**, and divided his government between them, Olympias seizing upon Epirus, and Cleopatra upon Macedonia. When Alexander was told of it, he said his mother had made the best choice, for the Macedonians would never endure to be ruled by a woman.]

Thereupon he sent Nearchus back again to the sea, determining to fill all the seacoasts with war. As he travelled through the countries far from the sea, he put his captains and governors to death which had revolted against him [*short omission*].

Part Two

As he came through the country of Persia, he first renewed the old custom there, which was that [when] the kings did return home from any far journey, they gave unto every woman **a crown** apiece. It is said therefore that for this cause, some of their natural kings many times did not return again into their country [*short omission*].

After that, **Cyrus' tomb (king of Persia)** being found and broken up, he put him to death that did it, although he was a Macedonian of the city of Pella (and none of the meanest), called Polymachus. When he had read the inscription written upon it in the Persian tongue, he would needs also have it written in the Greek tongue: and this it was:

> "O man, what so thou art, and whencesoever thou comest, for I know thou shalt come: I am Cyrus that conquered the Empire of Persia, [and] I pray thee envy me not for this little earth that covereth my body."

These words pierced Alexander's heart, when he considered the uncertainty of worldly things.

[*omitted: the suicide of Calanus the philosopher*]

When they were in the city of Susa, he married [off] certain of his friends, and himself also married Statira, one of King Darius' daughters, disposing also of the other Persian ladies (according to their estate and birth) unto his best friends. He made also a solemn feast amongst the Macedonians, of them that had been married before. At [this] feast, it is written that, nine thousand persons sitting at the boards, he gave unto every one of them a cup of gold to offer wine in honour of the gods. And there also, amongst other wonderful gifts, he did pay all the debts the Macedonians [owed] unto their creditors, the which amounted unto the sum of ten thousand talents saving a hundred and thirty less.

Whereupon **Antigonus with one eye**, falsely putting in his name amongst the number of the debtors and bringing in [some]one that said he had lent him money: Alexander caused him to be paid. But afterwards, when it was proved to his face that there was no such matter: Alexander then was so offended with him, that he banished him [from] his court, and deprived him of his captainship, notwithstanding that he had before shewed himself a valiant man in the wars. For when he was but a young man, he was shot into the eye, before the city of Perinthus, which King Philip did besiege: and at that present time they would have plucked the arrow out of his eye, but he never fainted for it, neither would suffer them to pull it out, before he had first driven his enemies within the walls of their city. [Accordingly, he was not able to support such a disgrace with any patience, and it was plain that grief and despair would have made him kill himself, but that the king fearing it, not only pardoned him], but bade him besides keep the money which was given him.

Narration and Discussion

What are some ways that Alexander showed that he still valued generosity?

Antigonus appears to have been a bit of a scoundrel. Why did Alexander let him off the hook?

For older students: Compare Alexander's reaction to the inscription about Cyrus to the previous discussion with the Gymnosophists. What may have been going through his mind?

Lesson Twenty-Three

Introduction

Alexander remained at Susa for a time, although Plutarch also mentions a trip to **Ecbatana**. He then prepared to travel westward to Babylon, not knowing it would be his last journey.

Vocabulary

thirty thousand boys: see **Lesson Sixteen**, Part Two

sick and impotent: those who were physically unable to serve

they let fall their stoutness: they let go of their stubbornness

naked in their shirts: this showed their humility

Ecbatana: a city in the Persian empire, located at an important crossroads of travel (where the Macedonians first saw naphtha)

sea Oceanum: see **Lesson Twenty-One**

dead hard by him: very close to him

tennis: this is North's translation; some sort of ball game

Aristotle's quiddities to argue pro and contra: Alexander, having studied with Aristotle, recognized his methods of argument

People

Antipater, Iolaus, Cassander, Hephaestion: see introductory notes

Historic Occasions

October, 324 B.C.: Death of **Hephaestion**

Reading

Part One

[The **thirty thousand boys**, whom he left behind him to be taught and disciplined, were so improved at his return (to Persia), both in strength and beauty, and (they) performed their exercises with such dexterity and wonderful agility], that Alexander rejoiced when he saw them. This, notwithstanding, did much discourage the Macedonians, and made them greatly afraid, because they thought that from

Alexander

henceforth the king would make less account of them.

For when Alexander would have sent the **sick and impotent** persons, which had been maimed in the wars, into the low country, to the seaside: they answered him, that so doing he should do them great wrong, to send these poor men from him in that sort (after they had done him all the service they could) home to their country and friends, in worse case than he took them from thence. And therefore, they said, if he would send away some, let him send them all away as men unserviceable, specially since he had now such goodly young dancers about him with whom he might go conquer the world.

Alexander was marvellously offended with their proud words, insomuch that in his anger he reviled them all, put away his ordinary guard, and took Persians in their place, making some the guard about his own person, [and] others his ushers, heralds, and ministers to execute his will and commandment.

The poor Macedonians, seeing Alexander thus waited on, and themselves so shamefully rejected, **they let fall their stoutness**, and after they had communed of the matter together, they were ready to tear themselves for spite and malice. In fine when they had laid their heads together, they consented to go unto his tent and without weapons, **naked in their shirts** to yield themselves unto him, weeping and howling, beseeching him to do with them what pleased him, and to use them like wretched unthankful creatures.

But Alexander, though his anger was now somewhat pacified, did not receive them the first time; neither did they also go their ways, but remained there two days and nights together, in this pitiful state, before the door of his tent, lamenting unto him, and calling him their sovereign and king: until that he came himself out of his tent the third day, and seeing the poor wretches in this grievous and pitiful state, he himself fell a-weeping a long time. So, after he had a little rebuked them, he called them courteously, and gave the impotent and sick persons leave to depart home, rewarding them very honourably. Furthermore, he wrote unto Antipater his lieutenant that he should always give them the highest place in all common sports and assemblies, and that they should be crowned with garlands of flowers. Moreover, he commanded that the orphans whose parents were slain in the wars should receive the pay of their fathers.

Part Two

After Alexander was come unto the city of **Ecbatana**, in the kingdom of Media, and that he had dispatched his weightiest causes: he gave himself again unto public sports, feasts, and pastimes, for that there were newly come unto him, out of Greece, three thousand excellent masters and devisers of such sports. [But they were soon interrupted by **Hephaestion's** falling sick of a fever, in which, being a young man and a soldier too, he could not confine himself to so exact a diet as was necessary.] Having spied opportunity that his physician Glaucus was gone unto the theatre to see the sports and pastimes, he went to dinner, and [ate] a roasted capon whole, and drank a great potful of wine, which he had caused to be set in water: whereupon his fever took him so sorely that he lived not long after.

[omission for length: Alexander's grief at the death of his friend]

Now as he was ready to take his journey to go unto Babylon, Nearchus his admiral came again unto him from the great **sea Oceanum**, by the river of Euphrates, and told him how certain Chaldean soothsayers came unto him, who did warn him that he should not go into Babylon. Howbeit, Alexander made no reckoning of it but went on. But when he came hard to the walls of Babylon, he saw a great number of crows fighting and killing one of another, and some of them fell down **dead hard by him**. Afterwards [it] being told him that Apollodorus, the governor of the city of Babylon, having sacrificed unto the gods to know what should happen to him: he sent for the soothsayer Pythagoras, to know of him if it were true. The soothsayer denied it not. Then Alexander asked him what signs he had in the sacrifice. He answered, that [the liver was defective in its lobe]. "O gods," said Alexander then, "this is an ill sign." Notwithstanding, he did Pythagoras no hurt, [but was sorry that he had neglected Nearchus' advice, and stayed for the most part outside the town, removing his tent from place to place, and sailing up and down the Euphrates].

Yet had he many other ill signs and tokens one upon another that made him afraid. For there was a tame ass that killed one of the greatest and goodliest lions in all Babylon with one of his feet. Another time Alexander had put off his clothes, to be anointed to play at **tennis**.

Alexander

When he should put on his apparel again, the young gentleman that played with him found a man [clad in the king's robes, with a diadem upon his head, sitting silently upon his throne]. Then they asked him what he was? It was long before he made them answer, but at the length coming to himself, he said his name was Dionysius, born in Messina: and being accused for certain crimes committed, he was sent from the sea thither, where he had been a long time prisoner, and also that the god Serapis had appeared unto him, and undone his irons, and that he commanded him to take the king's gown and his diadem, and to sit him down in his chair of estate, and say never a word. When Alexander heard it, he put him to death according to the counsel of his soothsayers: but then his mind was troubled. [He] feared that the gods had forsaken him, and [he] also grew to suspect his friends.

But first of all, Alexander feared **Antipater** and his sons, above all other. For one of them called **Iolaus**, was his first cupbearer: and his brother called **Cassander**, was newly come out of Greece unto him. The first time that Cassander saw some of the barbarous people reverencing Alexander, he having been brought up with the [manners] of Greece, and had never seen the like before: [he] fell into a loud laughing, very unreverently. Therewith King Alexander was so offended, that he took him by the hair of his head with both his hands and knocked his head and the wall together.

Another time also when Cassander did answer some that accused his father Antipater: King Alexander took him up sharply and said unto him: "What sayest thou?" said he. "Dost thou think that these men would have gone [on] so long a journey as this, falsely to accuse thy father, if he had not done them wrong?" Cassander again replied unto Alexander, and said, that that was a manifest proof of their false accusation, for that they did now accuse him being so far off, because they thought they could not suddenly be disproved. Alexander [smiled], and said, "Lo, these are **Aristotle's quiddities to argue pro and contra**: but this will not save you from punishment, if I find that you have done these men wrong."

In fine, they report that Cassander took such an inward fear and conceit upon it, that long time after when he was king of Macedon, and had all Greece at his commandment: going up and down the city of Delphi, and beholding the monuments and images that are there, he found one of Alexander, which put him into such a sudden fear that the hairs of his head stood upright, and his body quaked in such sort, that it was a great time before he could come to himself again.

Narration and Discussion

Why did the successful training of the Persian boys create such jealousy among the Macedonians?

Did Alexander seem particularly worried by the string of "bad omens?"

For older students: "They answered him, that so doing he should do them great wrong, to send these poor men from him…" Why were Alexander's soldiers so angry with him for suggesting what might seem a humane gesture, sending the wounded away to recover? How can "helping" sometimes be misapplied or misunderstood?

Lesson Twenty-Four

Introduction

This lesson describes the sudden and final illness of Alexander, at the age of thirty-two. The cause of his death has been attributed to everything from alcohol to typhoid fever to poison; but it seems to be a mystery that will never be solved.

Vocabulary

an ague: a fever

all at a draught: in one gulp

fell a-raving: became delirious

the thirti[eth] day: Plutarch's dates do not match those stated elsewhere, and seem inconsistent even within the text

watch and ward without: keep guard outside

Alexander

People

Perdiccas, Arrhidaeus: see introductory notes

Historic Occasions

323 B.C.: the death of Alexander in Babylon

Reading

Part One

[When once Alexander had given way to fears of supernatural influence], his mind was so troubled and afraid, that no strange thing happened unto him, how little soever it was, but he took it straight for a sign and prediction from the gods: so that his tent was always full of priests and soothsayers that did nothing but sacrifice and purify and tend unto divinements. So horrible a thing is the mistrust and contempt of the gods, when it is begotten in the hearts of men, and superstition also so dreadful, that it filleth the guilty consciences and fearful hearts like water distilling from above: as at that time it filled Alexander with all folly, after that fear had once possessed him.

This notwithstanding, after that he had received some answers touching Hephaestion from the oracle of Jupiter Ammon, he left his sorrow, and returned again to his banquets and feasting. For he did sumptuously feast Nearchus, and one day when he came out of his bath according to his manner, being ready to go to bed, Medius (one of his captains) besought him to come to a banquet to him at his lodging. Alexander went thither and drank there all that night and the next day, so that he got **an ague** by it. But that came not (as some write) by drinking up Hercules' cup **all at a draught**: neither for the sudden pain he felt between his shoulders, as if he had been thrust into the back with a spear. For all these were thought to be written, by some, for lies and fables, because they would have made the end of this great tragedy lamentable and pitiful. But Aristobulus writeth, that he had such an extreme fever and thirst withal, that he drank wine, and after that **fell a-raving**, and at the length died **the thirti[eth] day** of the month of June.

The Plutarch Project

[*These are the details of his illness.*] In his household book of things passed daily, it is written, that his fever being upon him, he slept in his hothouse [Dryden: *in the bathing-room*] on the eighteenth day of June. The next morning after he was come out of his hothouse, he went into his chamber, and passed all that day playing at dice: and at night very late, after he had bathed himself and sacrificed unto the gods, he fell to meat, and had his fever that night. And the twent[ieth] day also, bathing himself again, and making his ordinary sacrifice to the gods, [he lay in the bathing-room], harkening unto Nearchus that told him strange things he had seen in the great sea Oceanum. The [twenty-first] day also having done the like as before, he was much more inflamed then he had been, and felt himself very ill all night, and the next day following in a great fever: and on that day he made his bed to be removed, and to be set up by the fish ponds [Dryden: *by the great bath*], where he [discoursed with his principal officers about finding fit men to fill up the vacant places in the army].

The [twenty-third] day [Dryden: *the twenty-fourth*], having an extreme fever upon him, he was carried unto the sacrifices, and commanded that his chiefest captains only should remain in his lodging, and that the other meaner sort should **watch and ward without**. The [twenty-fourth] day [Dryden: *the twenty-fifth*], he was carried unto the other palace of the kings, which is on the other side of the lake, where he slept a little, but the fever never left him: and when his captains and noblemen came to do him humble reverence and to see him, he lay speechless.

So did he the [following day] also: insomuch as the Macedonians thought he was dead. Then they came and knocked at the palace gate, and cried out unto his friends and familiars, and threatened them, so that they were compelled to open them the gate. Thereupon the gates were opened, and they, coming in their gowns, went unto his bedside to see him. That [same] day Python and Seleucus were appointed by the king's friends to go to the temple of the god Serapis, to know if they should bring King Alexander thither. The god answered them, that they should not remove him from thence.

The eight and twent[ieth] day at night Alexander died. Thus it is written word for word in manner, in the household book of remembrance.

Alexander

Part Two

At [that] time, there was no suspicion that he was poisoned. Yet they say that, six years after, there appeared some proof that he was poisoned. Whereupon his mother Olympias put many men to death, and cast the ashes of Iolaus into the wind, that was dead before, for that it was said he [Iolaus] gave him [Alexander] poison in his drink.

They that think it was Aristotle that counselled Antipater to do it, by whose means the poison was brought: they say that Hagnothemis reported it, having heard it of King Antigonus' own mouth. The poison (as some say) was cold as ice, and falleth from a rock in the territory of the city of Nonacris, [which they gathered like a thin dew, and kept in an ass's hoof; for it was so very cold and penetrating that no other vessel would hold it]. Others defend it, and say, that the report of his poisoning is untrue: and for proof thereof they allege this reason, which is of no small importance: that is that the chiefest captains fell at great variance after his death, so that the corpse of Alexander remained many days naked without burial, in a hot dry country, and yet there never appeared any sign or token upon his body that he was poisoned, but [it] was still a clean and fair corpse as could be.

[Roxane, who was now with child, and upon that account much honoured by the Macedonians], did malice Statira extremely, and did finely deceive her by a counterfeit letter she sent, as if it had come from Alexander, willing her to come unto him. But when she was come, Roxane killed her and her sister, and then threw their bodies into a well, and filled it up with earth, with **Perdiccas'** help and consent. [Perdiccas, in the time immediately following the king's death, under cover of the name of **Arrhidaeus**, whom he carried about him as a sort of guard to his person, exercised the chief authority.]

[*brief omission*]

Narration and Discussion

In the introductory notes for this study, a teacher describes Alexander's "wisdom, valour, and self-reliance," and his "love of simplicity, generosity, and kindness to his men." She also suggests that Alexander had a gift of prudence, meaning (she explains) that he knew how to put the important things first. Did those traits accurately describe Alexander throughout his life; or did his values change along with events and circumstances?

Examination Questions for Term Two

Younger students

1. Why and how did Alexander teach his men to "acquaint themselves with hardness?"

2. How did Alexander go to war with King Porus? Give the whole story.

Older students (Choose two of these)

1. On what occasions were the following words used? Tell the whole story in two cases. (a) "If I drink alone, all these men will faint." (b) "Antipater," he said, "does not know that one tear of a mother effaces a thousand such letters as these."

2. How did Alexander talk with the philosophers of India?

3. "To live at pleasure is a vile thing, and to travail is princely." Why did Alexander thus rebuke his friends? Tell the whole story.

Timoleon
[ca. 411-337 B.C.]

Introduction

Timoleon was a Corinthian citizen who had given up public life after painful personal losses. Nevertheless, when the city needed someone to lead a military mission, he was the person suggested. Timoleon was exhorted (or blackmailed) into taking up the challenge; and from that time on, he became famous "not only for virtues, but for success."

The Setting

Syracuse was a Corinthian colony on the island of Sicily; the name refers both to the city and to the region it ruled. This may seem confusing since Sicily now belongs to Italy rather than Greece, but in the ancient world it was part of the region called Magna Graecia, "Great Greece." The Roman statesman Cicero, three hundred years later, called Syracuse "the most beautiful city in Magna Graecia."

Syracuse was ruled by **tyrant** kings (see below), most recently the cruel Dionysius the Elder (not part of this *Life*) and then his son, Dionysius the Younger (ca. 397-343 B.C., referred to here as **Dionysius**). To make things even more confusing, Dionysius (the

Younger) had been exiled and replaced by his former mentor **Dion** (the subject of Plutarch's *Life of Dion*); but he had ousted Dion and returned to power three years later. With a weak ruler and an unhappy colony, Syracuse seemed ripe for attack by other powers, such as neighbouring king **Hicetas** and the **Carthaginians**.

What is a tyrant? The idea of a "tyrant king" in the ancient world was somewhat different from the way we use the word "tyrant" today. It meant an absolute ruler, but it wasn't a judgment about whether he was good or evil. In this case, though, the "tyrants" had gone too far; so the Corinthians were asked to restore law and liberty to the colony.

Maps and Places

Most of the action of the story takes place in **Sicily**, the large island across the **Strait of Messina** from the mainland city of **Rhegium** (now Reggio Calabria) which is on the "toe" of Italy's "boot." **Syracuse** was/is located near the southeastern corner of the island. The "fort" or "castle" of Syracuse was located on the isle of **Ortygia**, right across from the larger island.

The city of **Leontini** was not considered part of Syracuse but was subject to its rule. Its tyrant-king at the time was **Hicetas**. Another city of interest is **Catana** (also Catina or Catania), at the foot of Mount Etna, which was ruled by **Mamercus**.

Across the **Mediterranean Sea** (in present-day Tunisia) was **Carthage**, a powerful city peopled by **Phoenicians** who spoke the **Canaanite** language. There were also Phoenician/Carthaginian colonies on Sicily, such as **Lilybaeum**.

Although the story concerns a Greek colony, the only Greek city to note is **Corinth**, located on the isthmus between the northern and southern parts of Greece. The southern half is the **Peloponnesus**.

Timoleon's Good Fortune

It is no accident that Plutarch speaks of Fortune as if she were a character in the story. Fortune (or Fortuna) was a Roman deity, the daughter of Jupiter; her Greek equivalent was Tyche. A modern-day derivative might be "Lady Luck." Fortune did not equal random chance, however; her blessings were said to be tied to one's virtue.

Was Timoleon married? We are told in **Lesson Eleven** that he had a wife and children, and that he sent for them when he eventually settled in Sicily; but no more than that.

A note on translation and spelling

The translation used is Thomas North's with some help from John Dryden [in brackets]. I have added more than the usual number of clarifying words, such as extra pronouns [also in brackets]. I have tried to use the most common spellings for names and places.

Top Ten Terms in *Timoleon*

If you recognize these words, you're well on your way to mastering North's vocabulary. (They will not be noted in the lessons.)

1. **Choler:** anger, temper
2. **Divers:** several
3. **Footmen:** foot soldiers
4. **Kin:** family, relatives
5. **Mean (adj.):** lowly, without status
6. **Target:** shield
7. **Repair unto:** go to, turn to
8. **Stay:** delay, detain, stop
9. **Strange:** foreign. Soldiers that are **strangers** are foreign mercenaries (soldiers employed by any army that will pay them).
10. **Victuals:** food. A **victualler** is a food supplier or grocer.

Prologue to the Life of Timoleon

(included for older students)

It was for the sake of others that I first commenced writing biographies; but I find myself proceeding and attaching myself to it for my own; the virtues of these great men serving me as a sort of looking-glass, in which I may see how to adjust and adorn my own life. Indeed, it can be compared to nothing but daily living and associating together; we receive, as it were, in our iniquity, and entertain each successive guest, view—

"Their stature and their qualities,"

and select from the actions all that is noblest and worthiest to know.

"Ah, and what greater pleasure could one have?"

or what more effective means to one's moral improvement? Democritus tells us we ought to pray that of the phantasms appearing in the circumambient air, such may present themselves to us as are propitious, and that we may rather meet with those that are agreeable to our natures and are good than the evil and unfortunate; which is simply introducing into philosophy a doctrine untrue in itself, and leading to endless superstitions. My method, on the contrary, is, by the study of history, and by the familiarity acquired in writing, to habituate my memory to receive and retain images of the best and worthiest characters. I thus am enabled to free myself from any ignoble, base, or vicious impressions, contracted from the contagion of ill company that I may be unavoidably engaged in; by the remedy of turning my thoughts in a happy and calm temper to view these noble examples. (*John Dryden's translation*)

Timoleon

Lesson One

Introduction

Like Shakespeare writing a play, Plutarch begins the *Life of Timoleon* by setting the stage and introducing supporting characters. **Lesson One** shows why a main character exactly like Timoleon was badly needed. But Timoleon himself does not come onstage until he is forced to make an appearance (in **Lesson Two**).

Vocabulary

Before Timoleon was sent into Sicily: this is the main event of the story, but we are not going to hear about that quite yet

the state of the Syracusans: see introductory notes about **Sicily, Syracuse, Dion,** and **Dionysius**

at dissension: in disagreement

tyrant(s): see introductory notes.

usurped: taken over

dogged: relentless

commended the design: praised the intentions

Peloponnesus: see introductory notes

People

Timoleon, Hicetas, Leontines, Carthaginians, Corinthians: see introductory notes

Historic Occasions

411 B.C.: the birth of Timoleon (approximate)

397 B.C.: the birth of Dionysius the Younger (approximate)

357 B.C.: Dionysius the Younger deposed by Dion

354 B.C.: Dion killed and Dionysius returned to power

344 B.C.: the Syracusan appeal to Corinth

Reading

Before Timoleon was sent into Sicily, thus stood **the state of the Syracusans:** after **Dion** had driven out the tyrant **Dionysius**, he himself after was slain coming immediately by treason; and those that aided him to restore the Syracusans to their liberty fell out and were **at dissension** among themselves. By reason whereof, the city of **Syracuse**, changing continually [under] new **tyrants**, was so troubled and turmoiled with all sort of evils that it was left in manner desolate, and without inhabitants.

The rest of Sicily in like case was utterly destroyed, and no cities in manner left standing, by reason of the long wars: and those few that remained were most inhabited of foreign soldiers and strangers (a company of loose men gathered together that took pay of no prince nor city), all the dominions of the same being easily **usurped**, and as easy to change their lord.

Insomuch, Dionysius the tyrant, ten years after Dion had driven him out of Sicily, having gathered a certain number of soldiers together again, and through their help driven out Niseus [Nysaeus], that reigned at that time in Syracusa: he [Dionysius] recovered the realm again, and made himself king. So, if he was strangely expulsed by a small power out of the greatest kingdom that ever was in the world: likewise he more strangely recovered it again, being banished and very poor, making himself king over them who before had driven him out.

Thus were the inhabitants of the city compelled to serve this tyrant: who besides [the fact] that of his own nature he was never courteous nor civil, he was now grown to be far more **dogged** and cruel, by reason of the extreme misery and misfortune he had endured.

But the noblest citizens repaired unto **Hicetas**, who at that time as lord ruled the city of the **Leontines**, and they chose him for their general; not for that he was anything better than the open tyrants, but because they had no other to repair unto at that time, and they trusted him best, for that he was born (as themselves) within the city of

Syracuse, and because also he had men of war about him, to make head against this tyrant.

But in the meantime, the **Carthaginians** came down into Sicily with a great army [Dryden: *navy*] and invaded the country. The Syracusans, being afraid of them, determined to send ambassadors into Greece unto the **Corinthians**, to pray aid of them against the barbarous people, having better hope of them than of any other of the Grecians. And that not altogether because they were lineally descended from them, and that they had received in times past many pleasures at their hands: but also for that they knew that Corinth was a city that, in all ages and times, did ever love liberty and hate tyrants, and that had always made their greatest wars not for ambition of kingdoms, nor of covetous desire to conquer and rule, but only to defend and maintain the liberty of the Grecians.

[But Hicetas, who made it the business of his command not so much to deliver the Syracusans from other tyrants as to enslave them to himself, had already entered into some secret conferences with those of Carthage, while in public he **commended the design** of his Syracusan clients, and despatched ambassadors from himself, together with theirs, into **Peloponnesus**]; not that he was desirous [that] any aid should come from them to Syracuse, but because he hoped if the Corinthians refused to send them aid (as it was very likely they would, for the wars and troubles that were in Greece) that he might more easily turn [it] all over to the Carthaginians, and use them as his friends to aid him against the Syracusans, or [against] the tyrant Dionysius. And that this was his full purpose, and intent, it appeared plainly soon after.

Narration and Discussion

What are the reasons the Syracusans needed help? Why did they decide to seek help from the Corinthians?

Why was King Hicetas so eager to send his ambassadors to Corinth?

For older students: Plutarch describes Corinth as a place governed "not for ambition of kingdoms, nor of covetous desire to conquer and rule, but only to defend and maintain the liberty of the Grecians."

Some people might argue that any government will inevitably be ambitious to conquer and rule, or will take from rather than support its citizens, because "power corrupts." Do you believe that a government (of a city or a country) can be an example of integrity to its own people and to others? Are there any such examples?

An extra challenge: Read and reflect on the Prologue (found just before this lesson). Why does Plutarch consider it false thinking to limit our studies only to those considered "good?"

Lesson Two
Introduction

In this lesson we hear the story of the worst time in the life of Timoleon, which was caused to some extent by the love and loyalty he felt towards his **"rash, hair-brained"** brother. How far would he go to cover up Timophanes' errors, and excuse his selfishness?

Vocabulary

named: nominated

preferment: honour

Fortune: see introductory note

commonweal: the collection of Greek city-states, or, literally, the common welfare or benefit of his people

in his greenest youth: in his youngest days

rash, hairbrained man: someone unwise and impulsive

bare him in hand: made him believe

Argives, Cleoneians: people of other Greek cities

salve: mend, heal

sported: laughed, mocked

Timoleon

waxed warm: got heated up

murder he had committed: Timoleon did not kill Timophanes by his own hand, but he was held responsible for his death

took a conceit: got an idea

all access of company: all interaction with others

it is very requisite and necessary: it is required

considerately: with careful thought and consideration

People

Æschylus, Satyrus: men involved in the death of **Timophanes**)

Historic Occasions

Mid-360's B.C.: events leading to the death of **Timophanes**

356 B.C.: the birth of Alexander the Great (for comparison)

Reading

Prologue

Now when [the Syracusan] ambassadors arrived at Corinth, and had delivered their message, the Corinthians, who had ever been careful to defend such cities as had sought unto them, and specially Syracuse: [they] very willingly determined in council to send them aid, and the rather for that [Corinth was] in good peace at that time, having wars with none of the [other] Grecians.

So their only stay rested upon choosing of a general to lead their army. Now as the magistrates and governors of the city were naming such citizens as willingly offered their service, desirous to advance themselves, there stepped up a mean commoner who **named Timoleon**, Timodemus's son, a man that until that time was never called on for service, neither looked for any such **preferment**. And truly it is to be thought it was the secret working of the gods that directed the thought of this mean commoner to name Timoleon: whose election **Fortune** favoured very much, and [who] joined to his valiantness and virtue marvellous good success in all his doings afterwards.

Part One (a flashback)

This Timoleon was born of noble parents, both by father and mother: his father was called Timodemus, and his mother Demareta [Demariste]. He was naturally inclined to love his country and **commonweal**: and was always gentle and courteous to all men, saving that he mortally hated tyrants and wicked men. Furthermore, nature had framed his body apt for wars and for pains: he was wise **in his greenest youth** in all things he took in hand, and in his [old] age he shewed himself very valiant.

He had an elder brother called **Timophanes**, who was nothing like to him in condition: for he was a **rash, hairbrained man**, and had a greedy desire to reign, [it] being put into his head by a company of mean men that **bare him in hand** they were his friends; and by certain soldiers gathered together which he had always about him. And because he was very hot and forward in wars, his citizens took him for a noble captain, and a man of good service, and therefore oftentimes they gave him charge of men. And therein Timoleon did help him much to hide his fault he committed, or at the least made them seem less, and lighter than they were, still increasing that small good gift that nature brought forth in [Timophanes].

As in a battle the Corinthians had against the **Argives** and the **Cleoneians**, Timoleon served as a private soldier amongst the footmen: and Timophanes his brother, having charge of horsemen, was in great danger of being cast away, if present help had not been. For his horse, being hurt, threw him on the ground in the midst of his enemies. Whereupon part of those that were about him were afraid and dispersed themselves here and there: and those that remained with him, being few in number, and having many enemies to fight withal, did hardly withstand their force and charge. But his brother Timoleon, seeing him in such instant danger afar off, ran with all speed possible to help him, and clapping his target before his brother Timophanes that lay on the ground, receiving many wounds on his body with sword and arrows, with great difficulty he repulsed the enemies, and saved his own and his brother's life.

Now the Corinthians fearing the like matter to come that before had happened to them, which was to lose their city through default of their friends' help: they resolved, in council, to entertain in pay continually four hundred soldiers that were strangers, whom they assigned over to Timophanes' charge. He, abandoning all honesty and regard of the trust the Corinthians reposed in him, did presently practise all the ways he could to make himself lord of the city; and having put divers of the chiefest citizens to death without order of law, in the end he openly proclaimed himself king of Corinth.

Timoleon being very sorry for this and thinking his brother's wickedness would be the very highway to his fall and destruction, sought first to win him with all the good words and persuasion he could, to move him to leave his ambitious desire to reign, and to **salve** (as near as might be) his hard dealing with the citizens. Timophanes would give no ear unto his brother's persuasions.

Thereupon Timoleon then went unto one **Æschylus** his friend (and brother unto Timophanes' wife), and to one **Satyrus** a soothsayer (as Theopompus the historiographer calleth him, and Ephorus calleth him Orthagoras) with whom he came again another time unto his brother: and they three coming to him, instantly besought him to believe good counsel, and to leave the kingdom. Timophanes at the first did but laugh them to scorn, and [he] **sported** at their persuasions; but afterwards he **waxed warm** and grew into great choler with them. Timoleon, seeing that, went a little aside, and, covering his face, fell a-weeping: and [in the meantime], the other two drawing out their swords, [they] slew Timophanes in the place.

Part Two (the flashback continues)

This was straight blown abroad through the city, and the better sort did greatly commend the noble mind and [hatred of wrong that] Timoleon bare against the tyrant: considering that he being of a gentle nature, and loving to his kin, did notwithstanding regard the benefit of his country before the natural affection to his brother, and preferred duty and justice before nature and kindred.

For before, he had saved his brother's life, fighting for defence of his country: and now in [Timophanes'] seeking to make himself king, and to rule the same, he made him to be slain. Such [people] then as misliked popular government and liberty, and always followed the nobility, they set a good face of the matter, as though they had been glad of the tyrant's death. Yet still reproving Timoleon for the horrible **murder he had committed** against his brother, declaring how detestable it was both to the gods and men: they so handled him, that it grieved him to the heart he had done it. But when it was told him that his mother took it marvellous evil, and that she pronounced horrible curses against him, and gave out terrible words of him, he went unto her in hope to comfort her: howbeit she could never abide to see him, but always shut her door against him.

Then he, being wounded to the heart with sorrow, **took a conceit** suddenly to kill himself by abstaining from [all food]: but his friends would never forsake him in this despair, and urged him so far, by entreaty and persuasion, that they compelled him to eat. Thereupon he resolved thenceforth to give himself over to a solitary life in the country, secluding himself from all company and dealings: so as at the beginning, he did not only refuse to repair unto the city, and **all access of company**, but wander[ed] up and down in most solitary places, [full of anxious and tormenting thoughts].

And thus we see that counsels and judgments are lightly carried away (by praise or dispraise) if they be not shored up with rule of reason and philosophy, and [thus obtain strength and steadiness]. And therefore **it is very requisite and necessary** that not only the act be good and honest of itself, but [that it must proceed likewise from solid motives and a lasting principle, that so we may fully and constantly approve the thing, and be perfectly satisfied in what we do]; to the end we may do all things **considerately**.

[omission for length and mature content]

Narration and Discussion

How did Timoleon show much love, but perhaps not enough wisdom, in dealing with his brother's weaknesses?

"And thus we see that counsels and judgments are lightly carried away (by praise or dispraise) if they be not shored up with rule of reason and philosophy, and [thus obtain strength and steadiness]." Why should we avoid putting too much importance on others' praise or criticism? Compare Proverbs 12:15 with Prov. 17:4.

For older students: Those who have read about the assassination of Julius Caesar might compare it with the death of Timophanes. ("Not that I loved Caesar less, but that I loved Rome more.") How might this experience have coloured Timoleon's feelings (positively or negatively) about the later call for him to fight against tyranny?

Lesson Three

Introduction

As the Corinthians prepared to sail to Syracuse, letters arrived from the tyrant Hicetas, intending to persuade them that their help was not needed, or at least to point out that they could not be successful against the Carthaginians, so they would be putting themselves into needless danger by even attempting the mission. However, this attempt at discouragement backfired, and even those who were previously unsure about the need for their intervention were now convinced that it was the right thing to do.

Vocabulary

abash: humiliate

levying of men: gathering a team for the mission

two faces in one hood: he was two-faced, or double-dealing

wrought his feat: succeeded

made league and amity: made an alliance

if any of the Corinthians were before but coldly affected...: if any of the citizens had been lukewarm about supporting the mission

the element: the heavens

ceremonies of the holy mysteries: religious rituals

the castle: the fort

willed: this does not seem to mean "forced," but "strongly suggested"

for reward of his treason: Hicetas expected the Carthaginians to agree to his rulership of Syracuse (as well as Leontini)

overthrown the battle: overcome the defences

People

Dionysius: see introductory notes

Historic Occasions

344 B.C.: Timoleon led the campaign to restore liberty to Syracuse (at about the age of 67)

Reading

Part One

But to returnsuscribed again to Timoleon. Whether that inward sorrow struck him to the heart for the death of his brother, or that shame did so **abash** him, as he durst not abide his mother: twenty years after, he never did any notable or famous act.

And therefore, when he was named to be general of the aid that should be sent into Sicily, the people having willingly chosen and accepted of him; Teleclides, who was chief governor at that time in the city of Corinth, standing upon his feet before the people, spake unto Timoleon, and did exhort him to behave himself like an honest man and valiant captain in his charge. "For," said he, "if you handle yourself well, we will think you have killed a tyrant: but if you do order yourself otherwise than well, we will judge you have killed your brother."

Now Timoleon being busy in **levying of men** and preparing himself: letters came to the Corinthians from Hicetas, whereby [it] plainly appeared that Hicetas had carried **two faces in one hood**, and that he was become a traitor. For he had no sooner dispatched his ambassadors unto them, but he straight took the Carthaginians' part, and dealt openly for them, intending to drive out Dionysius and to make himself king of Syracuse. But fearing lest the Corinthians would send aid before he had **wrought his feat**, he wrote again unto the Corinthians, sending them word that they should not need now to put themselves to any charge or danger for coming into Sicily, and specially because the Carthaginians were very angry, and did also lie in wait in the way as they should come, with a great fleet of ships to meet with their army: and that for himself, because he saw they tarried long, he had **made league and amity** with them [the Carthaginians] against the tyrant Dionysius.

When they had read his letters, **if any of the Corinthians were before but coldly affected to this journey**, choler did then so warm them against Hicetas, that they frankly granted Timoleon what he would ask, and help[ed] to furnish him to set him out.

Part Two

When the ships were ready rigged, and the soldiers were furnished of all things necessary for their departure, the nuns of the goddess Proserpina said they saw a vision in their dream, and that the goddesses Ceres and Proserpina did appear unto them, apparelled like travellers to take a journey: and told them that they would go with Timoleon into Sicily.

[*omission for length: omens which foretold success for the Corinthians*]

He took ship and sailed with seven galleys of Corinth, two of Corfu [Corcyra], and ten [which] the Leucadians did [furnish]. When he was launched out in the main sea, having a frank gale of wind and large, he thought in the night that **the element** did open, and that out of the same there came a marvellous great bright light over his ship, and it was much like to a torch burning, when they show the **ceremonies of the holy mysteries**. This torch did accompany and guide them [during] all their voyage, and in the end it vanished away, and seemed to fall down upon the coast of Italy, where the shipmasters had determined to arrive.

[*short omission*]

Thus did this celestial sign of the gods both encourage those that went [on] this journey, and deliver them also assured hope, who sailed with all possible speed they could: until such time, as having crossed the seas, they arrived upon the coast of Italy. But when they came thither, the news they understood from Sicily put Timoleon in great perplexity, and [it] did marvellously discourage the soldiers he brought with him. For Hicetas having **overthrown the battle** of the tyrant **Dionysius**, and possessed the greatest part of the city of Syracuse, he did besiege him [Dionysius] within **the castle**, and within that part of the city which is called "the Island," where he had pent him up and enclosed him in with walls round about.

And in the meantime he [Hicetas] had prayed [to] the Carthaginians that they would be careful to keep Timoleon from landing in Sicily, to the end that, by preventing that aid, they might easily divide Sicily between them, and [have] no man to [stop] them.

The Carthaginians, following his request, sent twenty of their galleys unto Rhegium, among which Hicetas' ambassadors were sent to Timoleon, with testimony of his doings: for they were fair flattering words, to cloak [the] wicked intent he purposed. For they **willed** Timoleon he should go himself alone ("if he thought good") unto Hicetas, to counsel him, and to accompany him in all his doings, which were now so far onwards as he had almost ended them all. Furthermore, they did also persuade him [that] he should send back his ships and soldiers to Corinth again, considering that the war was now brought to good pass, and that the Carthaginians would in no case [allow] that his men should pass into Sicily, and that they were determined to fight with them, if they made any force to enter.

So the Corinthians, at their arrival into the city of Rhegium, finding there these ambassadors, and seeing the fleet of the Carthaginians' ships, which did ride at anchor not far off from them: it spited them on the one side to see they were thus mocked and abused by Hicetas. For every one of them were marvellous angry with him, and were greatly afeared also for the poor Sicilians, whom too plainly they saw [were] left a prey unto Hicetas **for reward of his treason**, and to the Carthaginians for recompense of the tyranny which they suffered him to establish. [For it seemed utterly impossible to force and overbear the Carthaginian ships that lay before them and were double their number, as also to vanquish the victorious troops which Hicetas had with him in Syracuse, to take the lead of which very troops they had undertaken their voyage.]

Narration and Discussion

How was Timoleon convinced to accept the mission to Syracuse?

Why was there such "perplexity" over the situation as they found it?

Creative narration: This is a good opportunity to do a little creative narration, either in the form of a news report, a journal entry, or a dramatization (live or on paper) of a meeting between Timoleon and his men to discuss the situation. What were their options?

Lesson Four

Introduction

Timoleon's "negotiations" with the envoys of Hicetas made it seem as if he was surrendring to their demands; but through a clever trick, he managed to escape from Rhegium and cross over to Sicily.

To his surprise, many of the towns (except for Tauromenium) were mistrustful of even Corinthian help, and they offered no co-operation. One city, Adranum, did want help against Dionysius, but the people were divided on which army to ask, so they invited everybody at once. On the way there, Timoleon's army ambushed Hicetas and his troops, and that victory brought them the full support of Adranum.

Vocabulary

> **conduce to his own security and discharge:** protect him and help him to carry out the task
>
> **made a countenance:** acted as if

haven: harbour

through the press: through the crowd

incontinently: without delay

his affection therein: his willingness to demonstrate that belief

Phoenicians: refers to the Carthaginians

and that shewing with speed: and without delay

lodged betimes: set up camp early

the vanguard: those at the front

out of order: unprepared to fight

javelin: spear

People

Andromachus, Mamercus: see introductory notes

On the Map

Tauromenium: a city on the east coast of Sicily (now Taormina), governed by **Andromachus**

Adranum: also on the east coast. Its people were the **Adranitans.**

Reading

Part One

[The case being thus, Timoleon, after some conference with the envoys of Hicetas and the Carthaginian captains, told them he should readily submit to their proposals (to what purpose would it be to refuse compliance?): he was desirous only, before his return to Corinth, that what had passed between them in private might be solemnly declared before the people of Rhegium, a Greek city and a common friend to the parties. This, he said, would very much **conduce to his own security and discharge**; and they likewise would more strictly observe articles of agreement, on behalf of the Syracusans, which they had obliged themselves to in the presence of so many witnesses. The design of all [this] was only to divert their attention, while he got an opportunity of slipping away from their fleet]; which the captains and governors of Rhegium did favour, and [did] seem to help him in: because they wished Sicily should fall into the hands of the Corinthians, and [they] feared much to have the barbarous people for their neighbours.

For this cause, they commanded a general assembly of all the people, during which time they caused the gates of the city to be shut: giving it out that it was because the citizens should not go about any other matters in the meantime. Then when all the people were assembled, they began to make long orations without concluding any matter: the one leaving always to the other a like matter to talk of, to the end they might win time, untill the galleys of the Corinthians were departed.

And staying the Carthaginians also in this assembly, they [the Carthaginians] mistrusted nothing, because they saw Timoleon present: who **made a countenance** as though he would rise to say something. But in the meantime, someone did secretly advertise Timoleon that the other galleys were under sail and gone their way, and that there was but one galley left, which tarried for him in the **haven**. Thereupon he suddenly stole away **through the press**, with the help of the Rhegians, [all of them] being about the chair where the orations were made; and trudging quickly to the **haven**, he embarked **incontinently**, and hoisted sail also.

Part Two

And when he had overtaken his fleet, they went all safe together to land at the city of **Tauromenium**, which is in Sicily. There they were very well received by **Andromachus**, who long before had sent for them, for he governed this city as if he had been lord thereof. He was the father of Timaeus the historian, [and] the honestest man of all those that did bear rule at that time in all Sicily. For he did rule his citizens in all justice and equity, and [he] did always shew himself an open enemy of tyrants. And following **his affection therein,** he lent his city at that time unto Timoleon, to gather people together; and [he] persuaded his citizens to enter into league with the Corinthians, and to aid them to deliver Sicily from bondage, and to restore it again to liberty.

But the captains of the Carthaginians that were at Rhegium, when they knew that Timoleon was under sail and gone, after the assembly was broken up: they were ready to eat their fingers for spite, to see themselves thus finely mocked and deceived. The Rhegians, on the other side, were merry at the matter, to see how the **Phoenicians** stormed at [having] such a fine part played them. Howbeit, in the end they determined to send an ambassador unto **Tauromenium**, in one of their galleys. This ambassador spake very boldly and barbarously unto Andromachus, and in a choler: and last of all, he shewed him first the palm of his hand, then the back of his hand, and did threaten him that his city should be turned over-hand, if he did not quickly send away the Corinthians. Andromachus fell a-laughing at him, and [he] did turn his hand up and down as the Ambassador had done, and bade him that he should get him going, **and that shewing with speed** out of his city, if he would not see the [keel of his ship] turned upward.

Part Three

Hicetas [was informed that Timoleon had landed in Sicily], and, being afraid, sent for a great number of galleys [from] the Carthaginians. Then the Syracusans began to despair utterly when they saw their haven full of the Carthaginian galleys, the best part of their city kept by Hicetas, and the castle by the tyrant Dionysius. And on the other side, that Timoleon was not yet come but to a little corner of Sicily, having no more but the little city [of the Tauromenians], with a small power and less hope: because there [were] not above a thousand footmen in all to furnish these wars, neither provision of victuals, nor so much money as would serve to entertain and pay them.

Besides that, the other cities of Sicily [did not trust Timoleon]. By reason of the violent extortions they had lately suffered, they hated all captains and leaders of men of war to the death.

[*short omission*]

Timoleon

[The only exception was the city of **Adranum** (consecrated to the god Adranus, and greatly honoured and reverenced through all Sicily)]; which was then in dissension, one [person] against another, insomuch as one part of them took part with Hicetas and the Carthaginians, and another side of them sent unto Timoleon. So it fortuned that both the one [Hicetas] and the other [Timoleon], making all the possible speed they could who should come first: [they] arrived both in manner at one self time. Hicetas had about five thousand soldiers. Timoleon had not, in all, above twelve hundred men, with the which he departed to go towards Adranum, [which was] distant from Tauromenium about three hundred and forty furlongs.

For the first day's journey, he went no great way, but **lodged betimes**; but the next morning he marched very hastily and had marvellous ill way. When night was come, and daylight shut in, he had news that Hicetas did but newly arrive before Adranum, where he encamped. When the private captains understood this, they caused **the vanguard** to stay, to eat and repose a little, that they might be the lustier and the stronger to fight. But Timoleon did set still forwards, and prayed them not to stay, but to go on with all the speed they could possible, that they might take their enemies **out of order** (as it was likely they should) being but newly arrived, and troubled with making their cabins and preparing for supper.

Therewithal as he spake these words, he took his target on his arm, and marched himself the foremost man, as bravely and courageously as if he had gone to a most assured victory. The soldiers seeing him march with that life, they followed at his heels with like courage. So they had Timoleon not passing thirty furlongs to go, which when they [had] overcome, they straight set upon their enemies, whom they found all **out of order**, and [the enemies] began to flee, so soon as they saw they were upon their backs before they were aware. By this means there were not above three hundred men slain, and twice as many more taken prisoners, and so their whole camp was possessed.

Then the Adranitans, opening their gates, yielded unto Timoleon, declaring unto him with great fear, and no less wonder, how at the very time when he gave charge upon the enemies, the doors of the temple of their god opened of themselves, and that the **javelin** which the image of their god did hold in his hand, did shake at the very end where the iron head was, and how all his face was seen to sweat.

This (in my opinion) did not only signify the victory he [Timoleon] had gotten at that time, but all the notable exploits he did afterwards, unto the which, this first encounter gave a happy beginning. For immediately after, many cities sent unto Timoleon to join in league with him. And **Mamercus** the tyrant of Catana, a soldier, and very full of money, did also seek his friendship.

Narration and Discussion

Tell all as you can about **Andromachus**. As a creative narration, you could include opinions and examples of his honesty and good leadership from his friends, servants, etc.

How did Timoleon lead his troops to victory over Hicetas, although they were outnumbered?

Creative narration: Those studying in groups might enjoy acting out the assembly scene in Rhegium, where the whole purpose of the assembly was to delay the envoys and prevent them from leaving the building, while Timoleon found the right moment to escape.

Lesson Five

Introduction

The first part of this lesson describes the surrender of Dionysius to the Corinthians, after the victory over Hicetas. The rest is a sort of sidebar to the main story: it's about the banishment of Dionysius to Corinth, and what he did there (such as having dinner with Philip of Macedon and chatting with Diogenes the philosopher). Dionysius, unfortunately, did not live long after these events.

Vocabulary

[he] made no more reckoning: he paid no more attention

advertise: inform

munition of wars: weapons

engines of battery: machines such as catapults

threescore and ten: seventy

rehearsed: already mentioned

the less regarded: less esteemed (and therefore less of a threat)

feigned: pretended

their most familiars: their best friends

when thou goest hence: when you leave

let: prevent

People

> **Plato:** one of the most famous Greek philosophers. **Dion** had studied with him in Syracuse years before and had brought him to the court again to mentor young **Dionysius**; but things had worked out badly between them, so it is not surprising that they did not meet again.
>
> **Philip [the] king of Macedon:** the father of Alexander the Great
>
> **Diogenes of Sinope:** (412 or 404 B.C.-323 B.C.), one of the founders of Cynic philosophy. This is the same Diogenes who met Alexander the Great in Corinth (*Life of Alexander*, **Lesson Three**).

Historic Occasions

> **343 B.C.:** the surrender (and later the death) of Dionysius

Reading

Part One

Furthermore, Dionysius, tyrant of Syracuse, being weary to follow hope any longer, and finding himself in manner forced unto it by [the] long continuance of [the] siege: **[he] made no more reckoning** of Hicetas, when he knew that he [Hicetas] was so shamefully overthrown. And contrariwise, much esteeming Timoleon's valiantness, he [found means] to **advertise** him that he was contented to yield himself and the castle into the hands of the Corinthians.

[Timoleon, gladly embracing this unlooked-for advantage], sent Euclides and Telemachus, two captains of the Corinthians, to take possession of the castle, with four hundred men: not all at a time, nor openly (for it was unpossible, the enemies lying in wait in the haven); but by small companies, and by stealth, he conveyed them all into the castle. So the soldiers possessed the castle, and the tyrant's palace, with all the moveables and **munition of wars** [that were] within the same. There were a great number of horse[s] of service, [a] great store of staves and weapons offensive of all sorts, and **engines of battery** to shoot far off, and sundry other weapons of defence, that had been gathered together of long time to arm **threescore and ten** thousand men. Moreover, besides all this, there were two thousand soldiers, whom with all the other things **rehearsed**, Dionysius delivered up into the hands of Timoleon; and he himself, with his money and a few of his friends, went his way by sea, Hicetas not knowing it; and so [he] came to Timoleon's camp. And yet within [a] few days after, Timoleon sent him unto Corinth in a ship, with [a] little store of money.

Part Two

[Dionysius] was born and brought up in the greatest and most famous tyranny and kingdom, conquered by force, that ever was in the world: which [he] himself had kept by the space of ten years after the death of his father. Since Dion drove him out, he had been marvellously turmoiled in wars by the space of twelve years: in which time, although he had done much mischief, yet he had suffered also a great deal more.

[*omission for mature content*]

Now when Dionysius was arrived in the city of Corinth, every Grecian was wonderful desirous to go see him, and to talk with him. And some went thither very glad of his overthrow, as if they had trodden him down with their feet, whom fortune had overthrown, so bitterly did they hate him. Other[s], pitying him in their hearts to see so great a change, did behold him as it were with a certain compassion, considering what great power secret and divine causes have over men's weakness and frailty, and those things that daily passeth over our heads.

For the world then did never bring forth any work of nature or of man's hand so wonderful, as was this of Fortune. [Fortune] made the world see a man that, before, was in manner lord and king of all Sicily, sit then commonly in the city of Corinth, talking with a victualler; or sitting a whole day in a perfumer's shop; or commonly drinking in some cellar or tavern; or to brawl and scold in the midst of the streets [with common women]; or else to teach common minstrels in every lane and alley, and to dispute with them, with the best reason he had, about the harmony and music of the songs they sang in the theatres.

Now some say he did this because he knew not else how he should drive the time away, for that indeed he was of a base mind [*omission*]. Other are of opinion [that] he did it to be **the less regarded**, for fear lest the Corinthians should have him in jealousy and suspicion, imagining that he did take the change and state of his life in grievous part; and that he should yet look back, hoping for a time to recover his state again: and that for this cause he did it, and of purpose **feigned** many things against his nature [*short omission*].

Some notwithstanding have gathered together certain of his answers, which do testify that he did not [do] all these things of a base brutish mind, but to fit himself only to his present misery and misfortune. For when he came to Leucades, an ancient city built by the Corinthians, as was also the city of Syracuse, he told the inhabitants of the same that he was like to young boys that had done a fault. "For as they flee from their fathers, being ashamed to come in their sight, and are gladder to be with their brethren: even so is it with me," said he: "for it would please me better to dwell here with you, than to go to Corinth our head city."

Another time, being at Corinth, a stranger was very busy with him, (knowing how familiar Dionysius was with learned men and philosophers, while he reigned in Syracuse), and asked him in the end, in derision, what benefit he got by **Plato's** wisdom and knowledge. [As to] the benefit of it, [Dionysius] answered him again: "How thinkest thou, hath it done good, when thou seest me bear so patiently this change of fortune?"

Aristoxenus (a musician) and others, asking him what offence Plato had done unto him: he answered, that tyrants' state is ever unfortunate, and subject to many evils: but yet no evil in their state was comparable to this: that none of all those they take to be **their most familiars** dare once tell them truly anything; and that through [his untruthful friends' fault], he left Plato's company.

Another time there cometh a pleasant fellow to him, and, thinking to mock him finely: as he entered into his chamber, he shook his gown, as the manner is when [people] come to tyrants, to shew that they have no weapons under their gowns. But Dionysius encountered him as pleasantly, saying to him: "Do that **when thou goest hence**, to see if thou hast stolen nothing."

And again, **Philip [the] king of Macedon** at his table one day descending into talk of songs, verse, and tragedies which Dionysius his father had made; making as though he wondered at them, how possibly he could have leisure to do them: [Dionysius] answered him very trimly, and to good purpose. "He did them even at such times," quoth he, "as you and I, and all other great lords whom they reckon happy, are disposed to be drunk, and play the fools."

Now for Plato, he never saw Dionysius at Corinth. But **Diogenes of Sinope**, the first time that ever he met with Dionysius, said unto him: "O, how unworthy art thou of this state." Dionysius stayed suddenly, and replied, saying "Truly I thank thee, Diogenes, that thou hast compassion of my misery." "Why," said Diogenes again, "Dost thou think I pity thee? Nay, it spiteth me rather to see such a slave as thou (worthy to die in the wicked state of a tyrant like thy father) to live in such security, and idle life, as thou leadest amongst us."

[*short omission*]

So, methinks these things I have intermingled concerning Dionysius are not [foreign] to the description of our *Lives*; neither are they troublesome nor unprofitable to the hearers, unless they have other hasty business to **let** or trouble them.

Timoleon

Narration and Discussion

Why does Plutarch think that Dionysius deliberately played a bit of a fool in Corinth?

If you have had a negative impression of Dionysius so far (as a tyrant king and an enemy of Timoleon), do these stories about him give you a different view? Was he someone you would like to have known? (Details about his rather strange upbringing and education are found in the *Life of Dion*.)

For older students: Plutarch says that some Corinthians saw in Dionysius's life "what great power, secret and divine causes have over men's weakness and frailty, and those things that daily passeth over our heads." Dryden translates that as "a proof of the strength and potency with which divine and unseen causes operate amidst the weakness of human visible things." Would Christians agree with this viewpoint? (Example: the parable of the Rich Fool in Luke 12.)

Lesson Six

Introduction

The island fort had been taken by the Corinthians, but the rest of the city was dominated by Carthaginian troops, and food was getting low. However, Timoleon's "Fortune" seemed to be looking out for him.

Vocabulary

strange, wonderful: out of the normal course of things

set the Corinthians in such a jollity: pleased them so much

stay: wait

corn: grain, wheat

through the press: through the crowd

hard to: close to

recovered: reached

discover the treason: confess the plot

asunder: apart

conjunction: connection

their victuals waxed scant: their food ran low

straitly kept: tightly guarded

devised instruments and inventions: war machines

dispersed abroad by tempest...: the ships guarding the fort had been driven out of formation by the wind and waves

Acradina: a residential section of Syracuse (which still exists)

the compass and precinct: the boundaries

People

Mago, their admiral: a long-serving Carthaginian officer

Neon [the] Corinthian: Although we do not seem to know more about him than is told here, he was obviously an intelligent and courageous commander.

On the Map

If you have a large map (or can construct one), you might try laying it out flat during this lesson and moving characters or objects around to represent the various groups.

Thurians: those of the **Thurii** city/colony, on the Tarentine gulf

Brutians/Bruttians: their territory roughly corresponds to modern-day Calabria

Reading

Part One

But now if the tyrant Dionysius's wretched state seems **strange**, Timoleon's prosperity then was no less **wonderful**. For within fifty days after he had set foot in Sicily, he had the castle of Syracuse in his possession, and sent Dionysius as an exile to Corinth.

This did **set the Corinthians in such a jollity** that they sent him a supply of two thousand footmen and two hundred horsemen, which were appointed to land in Italy, in the country of the **Thurians**. And perceiving that they could not possibly go from thence into Sicily, because the Carthaginians kept the seas with a great navy of ships, and that thereby they were compelled to **stay** for [a] better opportunity: in the meantime, they bestowed their leisure in doing a notable good act. For the **Thurians**, [going out to war against their **Brutian** enemies, left their city in charge with these Corinthian strangers, who defended it as carefully as if it had been their own country, and (then) faithfully resigned it up again.]

Part Two

Hicetas all this while did besiege the castle of Syracuse, preventing [in every way possible] that there should come no **corn** by sea unto the Corinthians that kept within the castle; and he had hired two strange soldiers, which he sent unto the city of Adranus, to kill Timoleon by treason; who kept no guard about his person, and continued amongst the Adranitans, mistrusting nothing in the world, for the trust and confidence he had in the safeguard of the god of the Adranitans.

These soldiers, being sent to do this murder, were by chance informed that Timoleon should one day do sacrifice unto this god. So upon this, they came into the temple, having daggers under their gowns, and by little and little thrust in **through the press**, [so] that they got at length **hard to** the altar. But at the present time, as one encouraged another to dispatch the matter, a third person they thought not of gave one of the two a great cut in the head with his sword, [so] that he fell to the ground. The man that had hurt him thus fled straight upon it, with his sword drawn in his hand, and **recovered** the top of a high rock.

The other soldier that came with him, and that was not hurt, got hold of a corner of the altar, and besought pardon of Timoleon, and told him he would **discover the treason** practised against him. Timoleon thereupon pardoned him. Then he told him how his companion that was slain, and himself, were both hired and sent to kill him. In the meantime, they brought him also that had taken the rock, who cried out aloud [that] he had done no more then he should do: for he had killed him that had slain his own father before, in the city of the Leontines. And to justify this to be true, certain [men] that stood by did affirm, it was so indeed. Whereat they wondered greatly to consider the marvellous working of Fortune, how she doth bring one thing to pass by means of another, and gathereth all things together, how far **asunder** soever they be; and linketh them together, though they seem to be clean contrary one to another, with no manner of likeness or **conjunction** between them, making the end of the one to be the beginning of another.

The Corinthians, examining this matter throughly, gave him that slew the soldier with his sword a crown of the value of ten minas, because that by means of his just anger, he had done good service to the god that had preserved Timoleon. And furthermore, this good hap did not only serve the present turn but was to good purpose ever after. For those that saw it were put in better hope, and [they] had thenceforth more care and regard unto Timoleon's person, because he was a holy man, one that loved the gods, and that was purposely sent to deliver Sicily from captivity.

Part Three

But Hicetas having missed his first purpose, and seeing numbers daily drawn to Timoleon's devotion: he was mad with himself, that having so great an army of the Carthaginians at hand at his commandment, he took but a few of them to serve his turn, as if he had been ashamed of his fact, and had used their friendship by stealth.

So he sent hereupon for **Mago their admiral**, with all his fleet. Mago at his request brought a hundred and fifty sail, which occupied and covered all the haven: and afterwards landed three score thousand men, whom the army lodged, every man, within the city of Syracuse.

Then every man imagined the time was now come, which old men had threatened Sicily with many years before, and that [they had threatened] continually: that one day it should be conquered and inhabited by the barbarous people. For in all the wars the Carthaginians ever had before in the country of Sicily, they could never come to take the city of Syracuse: and [now] through Hicetas' treason, who had received them, they were seen encamped there.

On the other side, the Corinthians that were within the castle found themselves in great distress, because **their victuals waxed scant**, and the haven was so **straitly kept**. Moreover, they were driven to be armed continually to defend the walls, which the enemies battered, and assaulted in sundry places, with all kinds of engines of battery, and sundry sorts of **devised instruments and inventions** to take cities: by reason whereof, they were compelled also to divide themselves into many companies. Nevertheless, Timoleon, [from] without, gave them all the aid he could possible, sending them corn from Catana in little fisher boats and small [skiffs], which got into the castle many times, but specially in storm and foul weather, passing by the galleys of the barbarous people that lay scatteringly one from another, **dispersed abroad by tempest and great billows of the sea**. But Mago and Hicetas, finding [out about] this, determined to go take the city of Catana, from whence those of the castle of Syracuse were victualled: and taking with them the best soldiers of all their army, they departed from Syracuse, and sailed towards Catana.

Part Four

Now in the mean space, **Neon [the] Corinthian**, captain of all those that were within the castle, perceiving the enemies within the city kept but slender [guard]: made a sudden sally out upon them, and taking them unawares, slew a great number at the first charge, and drove away the other. So by this occasion he [Neon] won a quarter of the city which they call **Acradina**, [which] was the best part of the city, [and that which] had received [the] least hurt. (For the city of Syracuse seemeth to be built of many towns joined together.) So having found there great plenty of corn, gold, and silver, he would not forsake that quarter no more, nor return again into the castle: but fortifying with all diligence **the compass and precinct** of the same, and joining it unto the castle with certain fortifications he built up in haste, he determined to keep both the one and the other.

Now were Mago and Hicetas very near unto Catana, when a post overtook them, purposely sent from Syracuse unto them: who brought them news that the Acradina was taken. Whereat they both wondered, and returned back again with all speed possible (having failed of their purpose at Catana) to keep that [which] they had yet left in their hands.

Narration and Discussion

Give some reasons that people thought Timoleon must have had some kind of guardian angel (or "Fortune") looking after him. Do you agree?

What person or group of people do you think showed the most courage or strength of character in this passage?

Creative narration: Pretend you are Hicetas writing in his journal, writing a letter, or singing the Leontine Blues. Tell how this has not all gone quite the way you wanted it to.

Lesson Seven

Introduction

As the battle for Syracuse continued, the Corinthian backup troops found a way across to the island (again due to Carthaginian lack of foresight). A campaign to discourage the Greek-born mercenaries working for the Carthaginians was also successful; but Hicetas was resolved to fight to the end, even if he had to do it alone.

Vocabulary

> **These successes, indeed, were such…:** The success of the previous events could be credited to the skill and courage of those involved, with nothing supernatural about it. What you will hear next, however, should have been impossible without the help of "Fortune." (See also the introductory notes)

Timoleon

that remained in the city of the Thurians: see **Lesson Six**, Part One

policy, device: trick

the Grecians that took pay on both sides: Greek mercenary soldiers, some hired by Timoleon and some by Hicetas and the Carthaginians

frequented familiarly together: fraternized, "hung out" together

commodious: full of good things

there was treason in hand: Mago suspected that his Greek-born mercenaries were secretly loyal to their own people, and that his life might be in danger

prayed him all he could to tarry: tried to persuade him to stay

hardly to be approached: difficult to access

People

Hanno: Hanno the Great of Carthage, who was not only a military leader, but one of its foremost citizens

Demaratus: a Corinthian military leader, appearing here and in **Lesson Nine**. It seems likely that he was the friend of Philip and Alexander mentioned in the *Life of Alexander*, **Lesson Thirteen**.

On the Map

Messina (in Latin, Messana): a city and its surrounding area on the Strait of Messina, in the northeast corner of Sicily

Reading

Part One

[These successes, indeed, were such as might leave Foresight and Courage a pretence still of disputing it with Fortune, which contributed most to the result.] But the thing I will tell you now, in my opinion, is altogether to be subscribed unto contention of

Fortune. And this it is.

The two thousand footmen and two hundred horsemen of the Corinthians **that remained in the city of the Thurians**, partly for fear of the galleys of the Carthaginians that lay in wait for them as they should pass (**Hanno** being [the Carthaginian] admiral); and partly also for that the sea was very rough and high many days together, and was always in storm and tempest; in the end, they ventured to go through the country of the Brutians. And partly with [the Brutians'] good will (but rather by force) they got through, and recovered the city of Rhegium, the sea being yet marvellous high and rough.

Hanno, [not expecting the Corinthians would venture out, and supposing it would be useless to wait there any longer], thought with himself that he had devised a marvellous fine **policy** to deceive the enemies. Thereupon he willed all his men to put garlands of flowers of triumph upon their heads, and therewithal also made them dress up, and [adorned his galleys with bucklers, of both the Greek and Carthaginian make]. So in this bravery he returned again, sailing towards Syracuse, and came in with force of rowers, rowing under the castle side of Syracuse, with great laughing, and clapping of hands: crying out aloud to them that were in the castle that he had overthrown their aid which came from Corinth as they thought to pass by the coast of Italy into Sicily; flattering themselves that this did much discourage those that were besieged.

But whilst he sported thus with his fond **device**, the two thousand Corinthians being arrived through the country of the Brutians in the city of Rhegium, perceiving the coast clear, and that the passage by sea was not kept, and that the raging seas were by miracle (as it were) made of purpose calm for them: they took seas forthwith in such fisher boats and passengers as they found ready, in the which they went into Sicily in such good safety, as they drew their horse[s] (holding them by the reins) alongst their boats with them. When they were all passed over, Timoleon having received them, went immediately to take **Messina**, and marching thence in battle array, took his way towards Syracuse, trusting better to his good fortune than to the force he had: for his whole number in all, were not above four thousand fighting men.

Notwithstanding, Mago, hearing of his coming, quaked for fear, and doubted the more [upon the following occasion]. About Syracuse are certain marshes that receive great quantity of sweet fresh water, as

Timoleon

well of fountains and springs, as also of little running brooks, lakes, and rivers, which run that way towards the sea: and, therefore, there are great store of eels in that place, and the fishing is great there at all times, but specially for such as delight to take eels. Whereupon **the Grecians that took pay on both sides,** when they had leisure, and that all was quiet between them, they intended fishing.

Now, they being all countrymen, and of one language, [they] had no private quarrel one with another; but when time was to fight, they did their duties, and in time of peace also **frequented familiarly** together, and one spake with another, and specially when they were busy fishing for eels: saying, that they marvelled at the situation of the goodly places thereabouts, and that they stood so pleasantly and **commodious** upon the seaside. So one of the soldiers that served under the Corinthians chanced to say unto [those that served the Carthaginians]:

> "Is it possible that you that be Grecians born, and have so goodly a city [*meaning Syracuse*] of your own, and full of so many goodly commodities: that ye will give it up unto these barbarous people, the vile Carthaginians, and most cruel murderers of the world? Where[as] you should rather wish that there were many Sicilies betwixt them and Greece. Have ye so little consideration or judgment to think that they have assembled an army out of all Africa, unto Hercules' Pillars, and to the sea Atlantic, to come hither to fight to stablish Hicetas' tyranny: who, if he had been a wise and skillful captain, would not have cast out his ancestors and founders to bring into his country the ancient enemies of the same: but might have received such honour and authority of the Corinthians and Timoleon, as he could reasonably have desired, and that with all their favour and good will?"

The soldiers that heard this tale, reported it again in their camp, insomuch they made Mago suspect **there was treason in hand,** and so [he] sought some [pretence] to be gone. But hereupon, notwithstanding that Hicetas **prayed him all he could to tarry,** declaring unto him how much they were stronger than their enemies, and that Timoleon did rather prevail by his hardiness and good fortune, than exceed him in number of men: yet he hoisted sail, and returned with shame enough into Africa, letting slip the conquest of all Sicily out of his hands, without any sight of reason or cause at all.

Part Two

The next day after [Mago] was gone, Timoleon presented battle before the city [of Syracuse]. When the Grecians and he understood that the Carthaginians were fled, and that they saw the haven rid of all the ships: [they] then began to jest at Mago's cowardliness, and in derision proclaimed in the city that they would give him a good reward that could bring them news whether the army of the Carthaginians were fled. But for all this, Hicetas was bent to fight, and would not leave the spoil he had gotten, but defend[ed] the quarters of the city he had possessed at the sword's point, trusting to the strength and situation of the places, which were **hardly to be approached**.

Timoleon, perceiving that, divided his army; and he with one part thereof did set upon that side which was the hardest to approach, and did stand upon the river of Anapus: then he appointed another part of his army to assault, all at one time, the side of Acradina, whereof Isias [the] Corinthian had the leading. The third part of his army, that came last from Corinth, which Dinarchus and **Demaratus** led, he appointed to assault the quarter called Epipoles. Thus, assault being given on all sides at one time, Hicetas' bands of men were broken, and ran their way.

Now that the city was thus won by assault, and came so suddenly to the hands of Timoleon, and the enemies being fled: it is good reason we ascribe it to the valiantness of the soldiers, and the captain's great wisdom. But where there was not one Corinthian slain, nor hurt in this assault: sure methinks herein, it was only the work and deed of Fortune, that did favour and protect Timoleon, to contend against his valiantness. To the end that those which should hereafter hear of his doings should have more occasion to wonder at his good hap, than to praise and commend his valiantness.

For the fame of this great exploit did in [a] few days not only run through all Italy, but also through all Greece. Insomuch as the Corinthians, (who could scant believe their men were passed with safety into Sicily) understood withal that they were safely arrived there, and [that they] had gotten the victory of their enemies: so prosperous was their journey, and Fortune so speedily did favour his noble acts.

Narration and Discussion

How did Hanno's trick backfire on him?

Explain the speech of the Corinthian mercenary to those fighting on the Carthaginian side. What was its unexpected result?

For older students: It might be interesting (strictly for fun) to take on the role of Fortune and have her describe (a bit boastfully) the part she played in these events. How does this relate to a belief in God's intervention vs. coincidence and good luck, or succeeding through one's own courage and skill?

Lesson Eight

Introduction

The Corinthians were now positioned to do whatever they wanted with Syracuse. They could install another tyrant king and control the region as they wished; but that was not their plan. With the support of the Corinthians, the Syracusans began to rebuild their devastated city.

Vocabulary

> **[the error of] Dion:** Dion, who had similarly seized the fortress to end the tyranny of Dionysius, had then taken it for himself
>
> **but went thither straight:** they all went right away
>
> **hard by the walls:** just outside the city walls
>
> **stout:** strong; some of these people had built isolated **castles** (or forts) for themselves, because they did not trust the government
>
> **barren:** empty, unused

besought: asked, pleaded with

defray the common charges: cover the expenses

statues or images: public statues

Reading

Part One

Timoleon, having now the castle of Syracuse in his hands, did not follow **[the error of] Dion**. For he spared not the castle for the beauty and stately building thereof, but, avoiding the suspicion that caused Dion first to be accused, and lastly to be slain: he caused it to be proclaimed by trumpet, that any Syracusan whatsoever should come with [pick-axes] and mattocks, to help to dig down and overthrow the fort of the tyrants.

There was not a man in all the city of Syracuse **but went thither straight**; and [they] thought that proclamation and day to be a most happy beginning of the recovery of their liberty. So they did not only overthrow the castle, but the palace also, and the tombs: and generally all that served in any respect for the memory of any of the tyrants. And having cleared the place in few days, and made all plain, Timoleon, at the suit of the citizens, made council-halls and places of justice to be built there: and did by this means establish a free state and popular government, and did suppress all tyrannical power.

[However], he saw he had won a city that had no inhabitants, which wars before had consumed, and fear of tyranny had emptied; so as grass grew so high and rank in the great marketplace of Syracuse, as they grazed their horses there, and the horsekeepers lay down by them on the grass as they fed; and that all the cities, a few excepted, were full of red deer and wild boars, so that men given to delight in hunting, having leisure, might find game many times within the suburbs and town ditches, **hard by the walls**; and that such as dwelt in **castles** and strongholds in the country, would not leave them, to come and dwell in cities, by reason they were all grown so **stout** and did so hate and detest assemblies of council, orations, and order of government, where so many tyrants had reigned.

[Timoleon, therefore, with the Syracusans that remained,

considering this vast desolation, and how little hope there was to have it otherwise supplied], thought good to write to the Corinthians, to send people out of Greece to inhabit the city of Syracuse again. For otherwise the country would grow **barren** and unprofitable, if the ground were not plowed. [And besides this, they expected to be involved in a greater war from Africa, having news brought them that Mago had killed himself, and that the Carthaginians, out of rage for his ill-conduct in the late expedition, had caused his body to be nailed upon a cross; and that they were raising a mighty force, with design to make their descent upon Sicily the next summer.]

Part Two

These letters of Timoleon being brought unto Corinth, and the ambassadors of Syracuse being arrived with them also, who besought the people to take care and protection over their poor city, and that they would once again be founders of the same: the Corinthians did not greedily desire to be lords of so goodly and great a city, but first proclaimed by the trumpet in all the assemblies, solemn feasts, and common plays of Greece, that the Corinthians having destroyed the tyranny that was in the city of Syracuse, and driven out the tyrants, did call the Syracusans that were fugitives out of their country home again, and all other Sicilians that liked to come and dwell there, to enjoy all freedom and liberty, with promise to make just and equal division of the lands among them, the one to have as much as the other.

Moreover, they sent out posts and messengers into Asia, and into all the lands where they understood the banished Syracusans remained: to persuade and entreat them to come to Corinth, [promising] that the Corinthians would give them ships, captains, and means to conduct them safely unto Syracuse, at their own proper costs and charges. In recompense whereof, the city of Corinth received every man's most noble praise and blessing, as well for delivering Sicily in that sort from the bondage of tyrants: as also for keeping it out of the hands of the barbarous people, and restored the natural Syracusans and Sicilians to their home and country again.

Nevertheless, such Sicilians as repaired to Corinth upon this proclamation (themselves being but a small number to inhabit the country) **besought** the Corinthians to join to them some other inhabitants as well of Corinth itself, as out of the rest of Greece: the which was performed. For they gathered together about ten thousand persons, whom they shipped and sent to Syracuse; where there were already a great number of others come unto Timoleon, as well out of Sicily itself, as out of all Italy besides: so that the whole number (as Athanis writeth) came to three score thousand persons.

Amongst them he divided the whole country, and sold them houses of the city, unto the value of a thousand talents. And because he would leave the old Syracusans able to recover their own, and [to] make the poor people by this means to have money in common, to **defray the common charges** of the city, as also their expenses in time of wars: the **statues or images** were sold, and the people by most voices did condemn them. For they were solemnly indicted, accused, and arraigned, as if they had been men alive to be condemned. And it is reported that the Syracusans did reserve the statue of Gelon, an ancient tyrant of their city, honouring his memory, because of a great victory he had won of the Carthaginians, near the city of Himera: [but they] condemned all the rest to be taken away out of every corner of the city, and to be sold.

[*omission for length: Timoleon's work to remove all traces of tyranny out of Sicily, and to re-establish the laws of Syracuse*]

Narration and Discussion

Show how Timoleon demonstrated wisdom in his dealings with the Syracusans. How did the people back in Corinth help?

Why didn't the Syracusans who "dwelt in castles and strongholds in the country" want to return? How could Timoleon relate to this?

How did the Syracusans raise money to restore their city? **Creative narration:** Write the thoughts of a Syracusan witnessing the sale of his favourite statue.

Timoleon

Lesson Nine

Introduction

Timoleon banished some of the former tyrants to Corinth; and he confined Hicetas to Leontini, under the condition that he stay out of military involvement. Hicetas and his allies were still determined to rule Sicily, however; and even more so when they heard that the Corinthians had moved into Carthaginian territory.

Vocabulary

sporting wars: casual attacks

their country: their territory

in midway: partway through the journey

he had that proof of them: they showed their true natures before he had to depend on them in battle

fell upon his army: met up with them

smallage: parsley or wild celery

took a conceit: got a notion

what number he would: as many as he could

vanguard: those at the front

paled in: hemmed in

on the flanks: on each side

People

(H)asdrubal and Hamilcar: Carthaginian generals

Demaratus: see **Lesson Seven**

Historic Occasions

340-339 B.C.: Hicetas persuaded Carthage to send troops to Lilybaeum

339 B.C.: Battle of Crimissus

On the Map

Lilybaeum: a Phoenician city on the western coast of Sicily; the site of present-day Marsala. The Phoenician name, translated as "Lilybaeum" in Latin, meant "Town that Looks on Libya."

Crimissus: possibly the Freddo, a river in northwestern Sicily

Reading

Part One

The Carthaginians on the other side, while [the Corinthians] were busy about [these] matters, came down into **Lilybaeum** with an army of three score and ten thousand men, two hundred galleys, and a thousand other ships and vessels that carried engines of battery, carts, victuals, munition, and other necessary provision for a camp; intending to make **sporting wars** no more, but at once to drive all the Grecians again quite out of Sicily. For indeed it was an able army to overcome all the Sicilians, if they had been whole of themselves, and not divided.

Now they being advertised that the Sicilians had invaded **their country**, they went towards them in great fury, led by **(H)asdrubal and Hamilcar**, generals of the army. This news was straight brought to Syracuse, and the inhabitants were so stricken with fear of the report of their army: that [although there were] a marvellous great number of them within the city, scant three thousand of them had the hearts to arm themselves, and to go to the field with Timoleon. Now the strangers that took pay were not above four thousand in all: and of them, a thousand of their hearts failed, and left him [Timoleon] **in midway**, and returned home again. [They said] that Timoleon was out of his wits and more rash than his years required, to undertake, with five thousand footmen and a thousand horse, to go against threescore

Timoleon

and ten thousand men: and besides, to carry that small force he had to defend himself withal, eight great days' journey from Syracuse. So, that if it chanced they were compelled to flee, they had no place whether they might retire themselves unto with safety, nor [a] man that would take care to bury them, when they were slain. Nevertheless, Timoleon was glad **he had that proof of them** before he came to battle. Moreover, having encouraged those that remained with him, he made them march with speed towards the river of **Crimissus**, where he understood he should meet with the Carthaginians.

So getting up upon a little hill, from whence he might see the camp of the enemies on the other side: by chance, certain mules **fell upon his army** laden with **smallage**. The soldiers **took a conceit** at the first upon sight of it, and thought it was a token of ill luck: because it is a manner we use to hang garlands of this herb about the tombs of the dead. Hereof came the common proverb they use to speak when one lieth a-passing in his bed: "he lacketh but smallage." As much to say, "he is but a dead man." But Timoleon to draw them from this foolish superstition and [ease their minds], stayed the army. And when he had used certain persuasions unto them, according to the time, his leisure, and occasion: he told them that the garland of itself came to offer them victory beforehand. "For," said he, "the Corinthians do crown them that win the Isthmian games (which are celebrated in their country) with garlands of smallage." And at that time also even in the solemn Isthmian games, they used the garland of smallage for reward and token of victory: and at this present it is also used in the games of Nemea. And it is but lately taken up, that they have used branches of pineapple [*Dryden says pine*] trees in the Isthmian games.

Now Timoleon had thus encouraged his men, as you have heard before: he first of all took of this smallage, and made himself a garland, and put it on his head. When they saw that, the captains and all the soldiers also took of the same and made themselves the like.

The soothsayers in like manner, at the very same time, perceived two eagles flying towards them: the one of them holding a snake in her talons, which she pierced through and through; and the other, as she flew, gave a terrible cry. So they shewed them both unto the soldiers, who did then all together with one voice call upon the gods for help.

The Plutarch Project

Part Two

Now this fortuned about the beginning of the summer, and towards the end of May, the sun drawing towards the solstice of the summer: when there rose a great mist out of the river that covered all the fields over, so as they could not see the enemies' camp, but only heard a marvellous confused noise of men's voices, as [if] it had come from a great army; and, rising up to the top of the hill, they laid their targets down on the ground to take a little breath. The sun having drawn and sucked up all the moist vapours of the mist unto the top of the hills, the air began to be so thick that the tops of the mountains were all covered over with clouds; and, contrarily, the valley underneath was all clear and fair, that they might easily see the river of Crimissus, and the enemies also, how they passed it over in this sort. First, they [the enemy] had put their carts of war foremost, which were very hotly armed and well appointed. Next unto them there followed ten thousand footmen, armed with white targets upon their arms: whom they, seeing afar off so well appointed, they conjectured by their stately march and good order, that they were the Carthaginians themselves. After them, divers other nations followed confusedly one with another, and so they thronged over [the river] with great disorder.

There Timoleon [considered] the river gave him opportunity to take them before they were half passed over, and to set upon **what number he would**. After he had shewed his men with his finger, how **the battle** [formation] of their enemies was divided in two parts by means of the river, some of them being already passed over, and the other [still] to pass, he commanded **Demaratus**, with his horsemen, to give a charge on the [**vanguard** of the enemy], to keep them from putting themselves in order of battle. And himself coming down the hill also with all his footmen into the valley, he gave to the Sicilians the two wings of his battle, mingling with them some strangers that served under him: and placed with himself in the midst, the Syracusans, with all the choice and best-liked strangers.

So he tarried not long to join, when he saw the small good his horsemen did. For he perceived they could not come to give a lusty charge upon the battle [formation] of the Carthaginians, because they were **paled in** with these armed carts, that ran here and there before them: whereupon they were compelled to wheel about continually (unless they would have put themselves in danger to have been utterly overthrown) and in their returns to give venture of charge, by turns on their enemies. Wherefore Timoleon taking his target on his arm, cried out aloud to his footmen to follow him courageously, and to fear nothing.

Those that heard his voice thought it more then the voice of a man, whether the fury of his desire to fight did so strain it beyond ordinary course, or that some god (as many thought it then) did stretch his voice to cry out so loud and sensibly. His soldiers answered him again with the like voice: and prayed him to lead them without longer delay. Then he made his horsemen understand that they should [draw off from the front where the chariots were], and that they should charge the Carthaginians **on the flanks**; and after he did set the foremost rank of his battle target-to-target against the enemies, commanding the trumpets withal to sound.

Narration and Discussion

Discuss the story of the load of smallage/parsley. How did Timoleon use it to turn his men from fear to courage?

Explain the strategy that Timoleon planned to use against the Carthaginians. How did he show skill in leadership, especially in dealing with the problem of the chariots?

Lesson Ten

Introduction

This lesson continues the story of the battle at the Crimissus River, and its aftermath.

Vocabulary

corselets, murrions: chest armour, helmets

fresh-water: inexperienced

stood the Grecians to great purpose: helped them a great deal

without any certain channel: without any proper outlet

recover: reach

entertain: employ as soldiers

stood not trifling: did not bother

environed: surrounded

made league: made an alliance

suddenly: quickly

People

Mamercus, Hicetas: see previous lessons

Gisgo: the son of Hanno the Great

Reading

Part One

Thus with great fury [Timoleon] went to give a charge upon [the Carthaginians], who valiantly received the first charge, their bodies being armed with good iron **corselets** and their heads with fair **murrions** of copper; besides the great targets they had also, which did easily receive the force of [the Syracusan] darts, and the thrust of the pike. But when they came to handle their swords, where agility was more requisite than force, a fearful tempest of thunder, and flashing lightning withal, came from the mountains. After that came dark thick clouds also (gathered together from the top of the hills); and [then] fell upon the valley where the battle was fought a marvellous extreme shower of rain, fierce violent winds, and hail withal. All this tempest was upon the Grecians' backs, and full before the barbarous people, beating on their faces; [it] did blindfold their eyes and continually tormented them with the rain that came full upon them with the wind,

Timoleon

and the lightnings so oft flashing amongst them, that one understood not another of them. [This] did marvellously trouble them, and specially those that were but **fresh-water** soldiers, by reason of the terrible thunderclaps and the noise [that] the boisterous wind and hail made upon their [weapons]: for they could not hear the order of their captains. Moreover, the [mud] did as much annoy the Carthaginians, because they were not nimble in their armour, but heavily armed as we have told you: and besides that, also, when the plates of their coats were through[ly] wet with water, they did load and hinder them so much the more that they could not fight with any ease. This **stood the Grecians to great purpose**, to throw them down the easier. Thus, when they were tumbling in the [mud] with their heavy armour, up they could rise no more.

Furthermore, the river of Crimissus being risen high through the great rage of waters, and also for the multitude of people that passed over it, [it] did overflow the valley all about: which being full of ditches, many caves, and hollow places, it was straight all drowned over, and filled with many running streams, that ran overthwart the field, **without any certain channel**. The Carthaginians being compassed all about with these waters, they could hardly [find their] way out of it.

So as in the end, they being overcome with the storm that still did beat upon them, and the Grecians having slain [many] of their men at the first onset, to the number of four hundred of their choicest men, who made the first front of their battle: all the rest of their army turned their backs immediately, and fled for life. Insomuch, some of them being followed very near [by the Syracusans] were put to the sword in the midst of the valley; others, holding one another hard by the arms together in the midst of the river as they passed over, were carried down the stream and drowned with the swiftness and violence of the river. But the greatest number did think by footmanship to **recover** the hills thereabouts; [but they] were overtaken by them that were light armed, and [they] put to the sword every man.

They say, that of ten thousand which were slain in this battle, three thousand of them were mere natural citizens of Carthage, which was a very sorrowful and grievous loss to the city. For they were of the noblest, the richest, the lustiest, and valiantest men of all Carthage. For there is no chronicle that mentioneth any former wars at any time before, where there died so many of Carthage at one field and battle, as were slain at that present time. For before that time, they did always **entertain** the Libyans, the Spaniards, and the Numidians in all their wars: so as when they lost any battle, the loss lighted not on them, but the strangers paid for it. The men of account also that were slain were easily known by their spoils. For they that spoiled them **stood not trifling** about getting of copper and iron together, because they found gold and silver enough.

[omission for length: the taking of much treasure]

Then Timoleon sent unto Corinth, with the news of this overthrow, the fairest armours that were gotten in the spoil: because he would make his country and native city spoken of and commended through the world, above all the other cities of Greece. For that at Corinth only, their chief temples were set forth and adorned, not with spoils of the Grecians, nor offerings gotten by spilling the blood of their own nation and country (which to say truly, are unpleasant memories), but with the spoils taken from the barbarous people their enemies, with inscriptions witnessing the valiancy and justice of those also, who by victory had obtained them. That is, to wit, that the Corinthians and their captain Timoleon (having delivered the Grecians dwelling in Sicily, from the bondage of the Carthaginians) had given those offerings unto the gods, to give thanks for their victory.

Part Two

Afterwards, **Mamercus** the tyrant of Catana, and **Hicetas** (whether it was for the envy they did bear to Timoleon's famous deeds, or for that they were afraid of him), perceiving tyrants could look for no peace at his hands: they **made league** with the Carthaginians, and wrote unto them that they should send another army and captain **suddenly**, if they would not utterly be driven out of Sicily. The Carthaginians sent **Gisgo** thither with threescore and ten sail; [and at] his first coming [he] took a certain number of Grecian soldiers into pay, which were the first the Carthaginians [had ever enlisted] in their service: for they never gave them pay until that present time, [but now] they thought them to be men invincible, and the best soldiers of the world.

Moreover, the inhabitants of the territory of **Messina**, having made a secret conspiracy amongst themselves, did slay four hundred men that Timoleon had sent unto them; and in the territories subject unto the Carthaginians, near unto a place they call Hierae, there was another ambush laid for Euthymus the Leucadian, so as himself and all his soldiers were cut in pieces. Howbeit the loss of them made Timoleon's doings [accounted all the more remarkable, as these [four hundred] were the men that, with Philomelus of Phocis and Onomarchus, had forcibly broken into the temple of Apollo at Delphi, and were partakers with them in the sacrilege; so that being hated and shunned by all, as persons under a curse, they [had been] constrained to wander about in Peloponnesus; when, for want of others, Timoleon was glad to take them into service in his expedition for Sicily, where they were successful in whatever enterprise they attempted under his conduct. But now, when all the important dangers were past, on his sending them out for the relief and defence of his party in several places, they perished and were destroyed at a distance from him, not all together, but in small parties; and the vengeance which was destined for them, so accommodating itself to the good fortune which guarded Timoleon as not to allow any harm or prejudice for good men to arise from the punishment of the wicked, the benevolence and kindness which the gods had for Timoleon was thus as distinctly recognized in his disasters as in his successes.]

[*short omission for length*]

Narration and Discussion

Describe the events of the battle at the Crimissus River in as much detail as you can.

For older students: Why did Timoleon seem to feel the killing of four hundred soldiers in Messina was no great loss? Do you agree?

The pieces of Carthaginian armour that the Corinthians sent back to Greece were given "inscriptions witnessing the valiancy and justice of those also, who by victory had obtained them." Dryden translates this "the noblest titles inscribed upon them, titles telling of the justice as well as fortitude of the conquerors." Can you explain this? Why was it significant that the armour was sent to adorn the temples?

Lesson Eleven

Introduction

Although a few diehard tyrants (Hicetas and Mamercus) continued to struggle against Timoleon, it was obvious even to them that they had lost their support.

Vocabulary

fell out: fought, argued

fording: crossing

pretenders: competitors

ancient: original, former

device: involvement; literally, his personal stamp

impute: credit

Historic Occasions

338 B.C.: the Carthaginians agreed to peace terms

338 B.C.: Battle of Chaeronea (for comparison)

On the Map

Calauria: a town in Sicily

Catana: see introductory notes

Agrigentum and **Gela:** cities on the southern coast of Sicily

Reading

Part One

[After this, while Timoleon marched to **Calauria**, Hicetas made an inroad into the borders of Syracuse, where he] carried away a marvellous great spoil. And after he had done great hurt, and spoiled the country, he returned back again, and came by Calauria to spite Timoleon, knowing well enough he had at that time but few men about him. Timoleon suffered him to pass by, but followed him afterwards with his horsemen and lightest armed footmen. Hicetas, understanding that, passed over the river called Damurias, and so stayed on the other side as though he would fight, trusting to the swift running of the river [and the height and steepness of the bank on each side, giving advantage enough to make him confident.]

Now the captains of Timoleon's bands **fell out** marvellously amongst themselves, striving for honour of this service, which was [a] cause of delaying the battle. For none passing over would willingly come behind, but [each man claimed it as a right to venture first and begin the onset; so that their **fording** was likely to be tumultuous and without order, a mere general struggle which should be the foremost. Timoleon, therefore, desiring to decide the quarrel by lot, took a ring from each of the **pretenders**, which he cast into his own cloak, and, after he had shaken all together, the first he drew out had, by good fortune, the figure of a trophy engraved as a seal upon it; at the sight of which the young captains all shouted for joy, and, without waiting any longer to see how chance would determine it for the rest], they began every man to pass the river as quickly as they could, and [fell to blows with the enemies, who were not able to bear up against the violence of their attack, but fled in haste and left their (weapons) behind them all alike, and a thousand dead upon the place.]

And within a few days after, Timoleon, leading his army to the city of the Leontines, took Hicetas alive there, with his son Eupolemus, and Euthymus, the general of his horsemen; who were delivered into his hands by [Hicetas'] own soldiers. [Hicetas and his son were then executed as tyrants and traitors; and Euthymus, though a brave man, and one of singular courage, could obtain no mercy, because he was charged with] certain injurious words he spake against the Corinthians.

[*omission: the murder by the Syracusans of the wives and daughters of Hicetas, in revenge for a similar act done against Dion. Mamercus (the tyrant of Catana) continued to conspire against Timoleon but was eventually caught and executed.*]

Part Two

Thus did Timoleon root all tyrants out of Sicily, and make an end of all wars there. [And, whereas, at his first entering upon Sicily, the island was as it were (had) become wild again, and was hateful to the very natives on account of] the extreme calamities and miseries they suffered: he brought it to be so civil, and so much desired of strangers that they came far and near to dwell there, where the natural inhabitants of the country [it]self before were glad to fly and forsake it.

For **Agrigentum** and **Gela**, two great cities, did witness this. [They], after the wars of the Athenians, had been utterly forsaken and destroyed by the Carthaginians, and were then inhabited again: the one by Magellus and Pheristus, two captains that came from Elea: and the other by Gorgos, who came from the isle of Ceos. And as near as they could, they gathered again together the first **ancient** citizens and inhabitants of the same: whom Timoleon did not only assure of peace and safety to live there, to settle them quietly together: but willingly did help them besides, with all other things necessary, to his uttermost mean[s] and ability, for which they loved and honoured him as their father and founder. And this his good love and favour was common also to all other people of Sicily whatsoever. So that in all Sicily there was no truce taken in wars, nor laws established, nor lands divided, nor institution of any policy or government thought good or available, if Timoleon's **device** had not been in it, as chief director of such matters: which gave him a singular grace to be acceptable to the gods, and generally to be beloved of all men.

[*short omission*]

Part Three

[For as the poetry of Antimachus, and painting of Dionysius, the artists of Colophon, though full of force and vigour, yet appeared to be

Timoleon

strained and elaborate in comparison with the pictures of Nicomachus and the verses of Homer, which, besides, their general strength and beauty, have the peculiar charm of seeming to have been executed with perfect ease and readiness]; even so in like manner, whosoever will compare the painful bloody wars and battles of Epaminondas and Agesilaus with the wars of Timoleon, in the which, besides equity and justice, there is also great ease and quietness: he shall find, weighing things indifferently, that they have not been Fortune's doings simply, but that they came of a most noble and "fortunate" courage. Yet [Timoleon] himself doth wisely **impute** it unto his good hap and favourable fortune [or the favour of Fortune]. For in his letters he wrote unto his familiar friends at Corinth, and in some other orations he made to the people of Syracuse: he spake it many times, that he thanked the almighty gods, that it had pleased them to save and deliver Sicily from bondage, by his means and service, and to give him the honour and dignity of the name.

And having built a temple in his house, he did dedicate it unto Fortune, and, furthermore, did consecrate his whole house unto her. For he dwelt in a house the Syracusans kept for him and gave him in recompense of the good service he had done dwelleth still them in the wars, with a marvellous fair pleasant house in the country also, where he kept most when he was at leisure.

For he never after returned unto Corinth again, but sent for his wife and children to come thither [to Sicily], and never dealt afterwards with those troubles that fell out amongst the Grecians, neither did make himself to be envied of the citizens (a mischief that most governors and captains do fall into through their unsatiable desire of honour and authority); but lived all the rest of his life after in Sicily, rejoicing for the great good he had done, and specially to see so many cities and thousands of people happy by his means.

Narration and Discussion

Describe the events at the Damurias River. How might it have ended badly? How did Timoleon handle the situation?

How did Timoleon plan to spend his "second retirement?"

For older students: Why did Timoleon give so much credit to Fortune and the gods for his success? Two Scriptures you might want to look up are Isaiah 45:1 and Acts 17:23.

In his comparison of Timoleon with Æmilius Paulus, Plutarch says "I would not intend any reflection on Timoleon for accepting of a house and handsome estate in the country…there is no dishonour in accepting; but yet there is greater glory in a refusal, and the supremest virtue is shown in not wanting what it might fairly take." Do you agree that it might have been more honourable to refuse the reward?

Lesson Twelve

Introduction:

Timoleon had to face a few harsh critics, but he handled them (as usual) with strength and grace. Plutarch ends the story with a description of Timoleon's final days in Syracuse.

Vocabulary

    convince him: convict him of wrongdoing

    adjournment: calling into court

    persuaded the Grecians unto: gave them this ideal

    peradventure: perhaps

    they dispatched it of themselves: they handled it themselves

    litter: a bed or seat carried by men

    propound the matter doubtful: explain the difficult problem

    razed to the ground: destroyed

People

    Laphystius, Demaenetus: critics of Timoleon

Historic Occasions

337 B.C.: the death of Timoleon (at about the age of 74)

336 B.C.: Alexander the Great became king of Macedon

Reading

Part One

But it is an ordinary matter and [a] necessity (as Simonides saith) that not only all larks have a tuft upon their heads, but also that in all cities there be accusers where the people rule. There were two of those at Syracuse that continually made orations to the people, who did accuse Timoleon: the one [was] called **Laphystius**, and the other **Demaenetus**. So, this Laphystius appointing Timoleon a certain day to come and answer to his accusation before the people, thinking to **convince** him: the citizens began to mutiny, and would not in any case suffer the day of **adjournment** to take place. But Timoleon did pacify them, declaring unto them that he had taken all the extreme pains and labour he had done, and had passed so many dangers, because every citizen and inhabitant of Syracuse might frankly use the liberty of their laws.

And another time Demaenetus, in open assembly of the people, reproving many things Timoleon did when he was general: Timoleon answered never a word, but only said unto the people that he thanked the gods they had granted him the thing he had so oft requested of them in his prayers, which was, that he might once see the Syracusans have full power and liberty to say what they would.

Now Timoleon, in all men's opinion, had done the noblest acts that ever [a] Grecian captain did in his time, and had above deserved the fame and glory of all the noble exploits which the rhetoricians with all their eloquent orations **persuaded the Grecians unto**, in the open assemblies, and common feasts and plays of Greece, out of the which Fortune delivered him safe and sound before the trouble of the civil wars that followed soon after: and moreover he made a great proof of his valiancy and knowledge in wars, against the barbarous people and tyrants, and had shewed himself also a just and merciful man unto all his friends, and generally to all the Grecians.

And furthermore, seeing he won the most part of all his victories and triumphs without the shedding of any one tear of his men, or that any of them mourned by his means; and [that he] also rid all Sicily of all the miseries and calamities reigning at that time, in less than eight years' space: he being now grown old, his sight first beginning a little to fail him, shortly after he lost it altogether. This happened not through any cause or occasion of sickness that came unto him, nor that Fortune had casually done him that injury: but it was in my opinion, a disease inheritable to him by his parents, which by time came to lay hold on him also. For the voice went, that many of his kin in like case had also lost their sight, which by little and little with age, was clean taken from them.

[*short omission*]

Now, that he patiently took this misfortune to be blind altogether, **peradventure** men may somewhat marvel at it: but this much more is to be wondered at, that the Syracusans after he was blind, did so much honour him, and acknowledge the good he had done them, that they went themselves to visit him oft, and brought strangers (that were travellers) to his house in the city, and also in the country, to make them see their benefactor, rejoicing and thinking themselves happy that he had chosen to end his life with them, and that for this cause he had despised the glorious return that was prepared for him in Greece, for the great and happy victories he had won in Sicily. But amongst many other things the Syracusans did, and ordained to honour him with, this of all other me thinketh was the chiefest: that they made a perpetual law, so oft as they should have wars against foreign people, and not against their own countrymen, that they should ever choose a Corinthian for their general.

It was a goodly thing also to see how they did honour him in the assemblies of their council. For if any trifling matter fell in question among them, **they dispatched it of themselves**: but if it were a thing that required great counsel and advice, they caused Timoleon to be sent for. So he was brought through the marketplace in his **litter**, into the theatre, where all the assembly of the people was, and carried in even so in his litter as he sat: and then the people did all salute him with one voice, and he them in like case. And after he had paused a while to hear the praises and blessings the whole assembly gave him, they did **propound the matter doubtful** to him, and he delivered his opinion upon the same: which being passed by the voices of the people, his servants carried him back again in his litter through the theatre, and the citizens did wait on him a little way with cries of joy, and clapping of hands, and that done, they did repair to dispatch common causes by themselves, as they did before.

Part Two

So, his old age being thus entertained with such honour, and with the love and good will of every man, as of a common father to them all: in the end a sickness took him by the back, whereof he died.

The Syracusans had a certain time appointed them to prepare for his funeral, and their neighbours also thereabouts to come unto it. By reason whereof his funeral was so much more honourably performed in all things, and specially for that the people appointed the noblest young gentlemen of the city to carry his coffin upon their shoulders, richly furnished and set forth, whereon his body lay; and so did convey him through the place where the palace and castle of the tyrant Dionysius had been, which then was **razed to the ground**.

There accompanied his body also many thousands of people, all crowned with garlands of flowers and apparelled in their best apparel: so as it seemed it had been the procession of some solemn feast, and all their words were praisings and blessings of the dead, with tears running down their cheeks, which was a good testimony they did not this as men that were glad to be discharged of the honour they did him, neither for that it was so ordained: but for the just sorrow and grief they took for his death, and for very hearty good love they did bear him.

And lastly, the coffin being put upon the stack of wood where it should be burnt, one of the heralds that had the loudest voice proclaimed the decree that was ordained by the people, the effect whereof was this:

> "The people of Syracuse hath ordained that this present body of Timoleon [the] Corinthian, the Son of Timodemus, should be buried at the charges of

the commonweal, unto the sum of two hundred minas; and hath honoured his memory with plays and games of music, with running of horses, and with other exercises of the body, which shall be celebrated yearly on the day of his death for evermore; and this, because he did drive the tyrants out of Sicily, for that he overcame the barbarous people, and because he replenished many great cities with inhabitants again, which the wars had left desolate and unhabited; and lastly, for that he had restored the Sicilians again to their liberty, and [allowed them] to live after their own laws."

[Besides this, they made a tomb for him in the marketplace, which they afterwards built round with colonnades, and attached to it places of exercise for the young men; and [they] gave it the name of the Timoleonteum. And keeping to that form and order of civil policy and observing those laws and constitutions which he left them, they lived themselves a long time in great prosperity.]

Narration and Discussion

Why did Timoleon say he was glad to hear criticism of his military actions?

In what ways did the Syracusans show their admiration for Timoleon?

For older students: As a citizen, what does it mean to "frankly use the liberty of [your country's] laws?"

A special challenge: In the prologue to the *Life of Timoleon*, which you will find in this volume just before **Lesson One**, Plutarch said that he treated the writing of someone's life much as receiving an honoured guest, "all that is noblest and worthiest to know." "Ah, and what greater pleasure could one have?" he said. Write your own impressions of Timoleon as Plutarch presented him. Is he someone you would "invite back" as valued company?

A possibility for debate: Who was greater: Alexander or Timoleon?

Timoleon

Examination Questions

Younger Students:

1. Why did Timoleon first save his brother's life and then consent to his death? Tell the whole story.

2. Give a short account of Timoleon's expedition against the Carthagenians.

Older Students:

1. Describe the conquest of Syracuse. How did Timoleon treat the city?

Bibliography

Plutarch's Lives of the Noble Greeks and Romans. Englished by Sir Thomas North. With an introduction by George Wyndham. Second Volume. London: Dent, 1894. (Timoleon)

https://archive.org/details/livesenglishedb02plut/page/n9

Plutarch's Lives of the Noble Greeks and Romans. Englished by Sir Thomas North. With an introduction by George Wyndham. Fourth Volume. London: Dent, 1894. (Alexander)

https://archive.org/details/livesenglishedb04plut/page/n9

Plutarch's Lives: The Dryden Plutarch. Revised by Arthur Hugh Clough. Volume 2. London: J.M. Dent, 1910. (Timoleon)

https://archive.org/details/drydensplutarchs02plut/page/n4

Plutarch's Lives: The Dryden Plutarch. Revised by Arthur Hugh Clough. Volume 4. Philadelphia: John D. Morris, 1860. (Alexander)

https://archive.org/details/plutarchslivestr04plut4/page/n6

A helpful book of maps:

Hyslop, Stephen G., and Patricia Daniels. 2011. *Great empires: an illustrated atlas*. Washington, D.C.: National Geographic.

About the Author

Anne E. White (www.annewrites.ca) has shared her knowledge of Charlotte Mason's methods through magazine columns, online writing, and conference workshops. She is an Advisory member of AmblesideOnline and the author of *Minds More Awake: The Vision of Charlotte Mason*, as well as other books in The Plutarch Project series.

Made in the USA
Columbia, SC
12 August 2020